AW^

HOW TO WATCH ^ ^UGBY

'One for all rugby lovers ... Spiro Zavos's best book yet'
Bryce Courtenay

'A compelling piece by one of today's great rugby
writers, capturing the romance and cultural depth
usually lost amid the mud and blood'
Justine Kirby, *Kiwi Klips*

'An exceptional writer ... Spiro Zavos's pieces invariably
challenge the thought processes of even the most
learned students of rugby'
John Eales, former Wallabies' captain

'Wonderfully compelling – an entirely new approach to
watching the game ... It makes you forget about inflated egos,
pedantic refs and overpaid prima donnas, and reminds you
what it was that attracted you to rugby in the first place'
Shannon Buckley, *Rugby News*

'Wry, thoughtful, erudite and, above all, amusing'
Warwick Roger, *North & South*

'Spiro Zavos combines a deep understanding of rugby ...
with wit, intelligence and flair'
Alexander Bisley, *Salient*

'Zavos would be the perfect person to watch footy with. Take this
book with you to the ground and consult it at critical moments'
Denis Welch, *Listener*

'Unveils the romantic side of rugby – a side most people
never knew existed'
Chris Laidlaw, *Radio New Zealand*

'A critical success with its humour, passion, anecdotes, analysis
and insight into what goes on, on and off the rugby field'
The Dominion Post

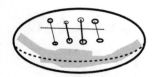

01

THE GINGER SERIES

OTHER TITLES IN THE GINGER SERIES

02 How to Gaze at the Southern Stars
Richard Hall

03 How to Listen to Pop Music
Nick Bollinger

04 How to Pick a Winner
Mary Mountier

05 How to Drink a Glass of Wine
John Saker

06 How to Catch a Fish
Kevin Ireland

07 How to Look at a Painting
Justin Paton

08 How to Read a Book
Kelly Ana Morey

how to watch a game of rugby
spiro zavos

AWA PRESS

First edition published in 2004 by
Awa Press, PO Box 11-416,
Wellington, New Zealand

Reprinted 2005

National Library of New Zealand Cataloguing-in-Publication Data
Zavos, Spiro Bernard, 1937-
How to Watch a Game of Rugby / by Spiro Zavos.
(The Ginger Series (Wellington, N.Z.))
ISBN 0-9582509-3-6
1. Rugby Union football. I. Title. II. Series.
796.333—dc 22

ISSN 1176-8452

Designed by Sarah Maxey
Cover illustration by Scott Kennedy
Printed by Astra Print, Wellington

The paper used in this book is environmentally friendly
and chlorine-free Munken

This book is typeset in Walbaum

www.awapress.com

For Judy

ABOUT THE AUTHOR

SPIRO ZAVOS, a first-generation Greek New Zealander, saw his first rugby test in 1949 at Wellington's Athletic Park when he was twelve years old and was struck with a lifelong passion for 'the perfect game'. He has written six acclaimed books on rugby, and his rugby column in the *Sydney Morning Herald* is a talking point for rugby followers on both sides of the Tasman. He lives in Sydney with his wife, teacher and children's book author Judy Zavos. The couple has two sons, Zolton and Zachary.

'Saturday afternoon in the Western Highlands, early autumn 1991, and not unusually I find myself lying in a corner of the Mushroom Field, seeped in the damp of the nearby Oban to Crinan canal. My cheek and eye are crushed into grass and mud, several half-naked strangers are piled at right angles beside and on top of me and softly, from the sea-grey sky, it starts to rain. Which is when I think, I seriously think: God, I love this game.'

Richard Beard,
Muddied Oafs: The Last Days of Rugger

Preface

'LOVE THE GAME!' could be the title of this essay: my contention is that the good watcher of rugby is the one who is passionate about the game. The good watcher cares about the play and the players. The eyes, the mind, the heart and, particularly, the emotions of the good watcher are engaged in what is happening on the field. He or she believes that a great game of rugby will take them out of their world and transport them into a better world for 80 minutes.

There is some discussion about the best place to sit in a stadium to watch rugby effectively. But it is taken as read that watchers will arrive early to a game to soak up the atmosphere, that they will wear warm clothing on cold days and that they will go to the toilet before the game begins. I put hints of this type in the category of how to be comfortable watching a game of rugby.

But you can be comfortable or uncomfortable, it doesn't matter, while you are watching rugby. One of the most dramatic tests I ever watched was between the All Blacks (5) and France (3) at Athletic Park on 5 August 1961. The winds were so ferocious the inter-island ferry was not allowed to try to enter Wellington Harbour. The ball could not be kicked forward into the howling gale. The test marked the opening of the Millard Stand, a steepling structure that virtually jutted out over the field from a great height. There were rumours that someone had been blown off. I was sitting nervously in the middle section and was not surprised by them. The southerly wind was so strong it seemed capable of lifting someone from the stand and depositing them miles away in downtown Wellington. Don Clarke kicked one of the weirdest and most wonderful conversions in test match rugby by using the velocity of the wind. Kicking from about 15 metres from the touch line, he directed his conversion at right angles to the goalposts. The wind, hissing and roaring like 100 steam locomotives, grabbed the ball as it left Clarke's boot and hurled it through the posts. No one watching the test was comfortable. But for everyone there it was a memorable occasion.

Real watching is not really about the externals. At its best, it is an internal experience. It is about a personal involvement with the play. The good watcher understands the spirit of the laws of rugby better than their details, knows something about the history of the game, treasures the great players and their deeds, appreciates the culture of rugby, and is loyal to his or her teams. The zen of rugby inhabits the soul of the good watcher. You can play rugby for a restricted number of years, or never play the game. The joy of watching rugby, though, is a lifelong pleasure open to anyone who is prepared to embrace it. Love the game!

'Rugby is a wonderful concoction of ballet, opera and bloody murder.'

Actor Richard Burton

Wonderful
concoction

On a blustery Saturday afternoon (it was Wellington, after all) in 1970, I trudged up to Athletic Park to watch the final All Blacks' trial to select a team to go to South Africa. With me was my partner and later my wife, Judy. The day before, I had met Chris Laidlaw in the Grand Hotel. There, in the main bar, with the cigarette smoke curling into the thick, beer-stinking air, with the good old boys in their cardigans and blazers leaning on the wet woodwork gossiping about who was going to be selected and who was out, he told me that he was determined to win back his All Black place from Sid Going.

Laidlaw had been at Oxford on a Rhodes Scholarship and Going was now the incumbent New Zealand halfback. They didn't get on well together, Laidlaw told me. Going, a wary Mormon, with a brilliant running game, was angry that the worldly Laidlaw, who was the best passing halfback of his or any other era, seemed to be returning to New Zealand like a prodigal son to reclaim his lost inheritance. The man-on-man battle between these two adversaries was one of the games-within-the-game I was interested in watching.

I was also intrigued about the eventual selection of the All Blacks. The coach, Ivan Vodanovich, was a good friend of mine. Ivan had come to Wellington from the King Country, bulked up, developed his scrumming skills and played for the All Blacks in the front row against Australia in 1955. After his playing career was over he had, as so many All Blacks had done over the decades, put his energies into administration and coaching.

I used to ear-bash him with theories about backline play (the fly half shouldn't start running forward until the halfback had actually passed the ball) and how a team should be prepared in the week of a big match. My theory here was that training should be tapered off, especially on the Thursday and Friday, so that players were full of energy, like a charged-up battery, on Saturday.

Ivan disagreed. The year before, he had trained the All Blacks relentlessly on the Friday before the test. It was so hot he had taken his jersey off and the sweat had poured down his massive chest as he yelled and needled the All Blacks into doing their drills with more and more pace and energy. The next day the All Blacks played a brilliant first half against Wales and then faded in the second as I had predicted, to win comfortably but not overwhelmingly, as they could have.

Missing from the trial squads was another friend of mine, Ken Gray. A thoughtful man, with brooding, sunken eye sockets and a sophisticated social conscience, Ken had walked down Manners Street one night before Christmas, when the streets were glistening with rain, and told me he was retiring because his detestation of the apartheid regime in South Africa was so intense he could not bring himself to set foot in the country, not even as a rugby player. He wanted to retire rather than make a statement about his unavailability on moral grounds. 'I don't want to embarrass Chris and Pinetree [Colin Meads] and Brian Lochore,' he told me.

Ken was the rock of the All Black pack of the late 1960s (one of the best teams New Zealand has ever put on to a field). Another of the intriguing questions that had to be answered during the trial was whether there was another player who could adequately replace him.

There were other questions, too. Who would be the bolter in the squad? Teams selected for major tours in this era often included players whose names elicited gasps when they were read out. Grant Batty, perhaps? Batty had been a brilliant schoolboy player. Earlier that year I had sat with the famous rugby broadcaster Winston McCarthy at Athletic Park and watched his debut as a senior. 'This boy,' McCarthy told me, in a voice that, in Tony O'Reilly's words, rasped like two mating pieces of sandpaper, 'is the most exciting New Zealand back since Bert Cooke.' As Cooke, a 1920s' All Black, is regarded as the greatest inside back New Zealand rugby has produced, the compliment was extravagant.

Ivan Vodanovich had told me that if Batty played through the trial, he would be selected. In fact, he limped off the field towards the end and had to be replaced.

There was some interesting off-field action to look forward to as well. A radical activist I had known at university had told the newspapers he was going to douse himself with petrol and set fire to himself on the half-way mark before the main trial as a protest against apartheid and the tour to South Africa.

The trial match, therefore, had many points of interest for the keen observer like me to watch out for. And as there is with every game of rugby, whether it is played on a suburban park with a handful of spectators, or at one of the great rugby stadiums with huge crowds, there was, as well, the theatre of the game and its tribal imperatives. Australian supporters screaming out, 'Tackle, Wallabies, tackle!' or New Zealand supporters singing out, 'Black, black, black!' (or, to un-Kiwi ears, 'Blek, blek, blek!') are sounds of a healthy society with its priorities right. It is much better to make tackles than to make war.

With all these emotions and thoughts roiling around in my subconscious, my heart was beating fiercely as the two trial teams, the Probables in black jerseys and the Possibles in white jerseys, trotted on to the clumpy, wind-swept grass of Athletic Park. At that moment, Judy bent down and pulled the latest issue of *Time* magazine from her bag. She steadfastly read her way through it while the players were vying for the prize of their lives and the spectators were going through emotional ups and downs with the fluctuating fortunes of their favourite players.

A month or so later, on the night of our wedding, a group of male friends joined me in the bedroom of our hotel to listen to (you don't have to be at the ground to 'watch' a rugby match) the radio broadcast of the second test between the Springboks and the All Blacks from South Africa. Chris Laidlaw had won back his halfback position, and played shrewdly and effectively to guide the tourists to a vital victory. We (the men) were ecstatic. Judy, though, was not amused.

This essay, then, is dedicated to all the Judys (men and women) who believe it is a waste of life's precious minutes to watch 'muddied oafs' throw themselves at each other in a rugby match. But it is also dedicated to all the rugby tragics like myself, the true believers, who know that 'one crowded hour of glorious life' is best spent at a match – any rugby match – either vicariously or physically, even on your wedding night.

'We see an object in the paint with which a surface is marked, rather than simply seeing the marks. One may see a spaniel in a spaniel in a painting by Landseer, for example, but one may also see a gleam of loyalty in the spaniel's eye: or discern heroism, optimism or nostalgia.'

Richard Wollheim, *Art and Its Objects*

An object
in the paint

ALL THESE subplots around Chris Laidlaw, Sid Going, Ken Gray, Ivan Vodanovich, Grant Batty, Bernie the activist and Judy, which all came together during the 1970 All Black trial, bring us to Richard Wollheim, a leading authority on the history of painting. For Wollheim's theory of how to look at a painting can be used as a general theory of how to watch a rugby match.

Wollheim argued that the good watcher must try to achieve a 'seeing in' of the objects in a picture. The good watcher, he said, sees more than the marks on the surface of the painting. He or she sees into the painting. Wollheim used the example of the good watcher who sees the 'gleam of loyalty in the spaniel's eye' in a painting by Landseer. The more knowledge the good watcher brings to the seeing-in process, the sharper and truer it becomes. The good watcher re-creates the painting with the various narratives they bring to the viewing.

A rugby match, according to this seeing-in theory, is never an objective reality. No one spectator sees the same match in the same way as any of the other spectators. The good watcher brings his or her personality and knowledge and passion to the game; the 'seeing-in' experience is therefore different from person to person.

The good watcher, in the arts world vernacular, 'subverts' the match. It becomes what the good watcher wants to see.

For my future wife Judy, for instance, that final trial was a doorway, opening into a world she might have to experience. But she did not have to stride through it this time. For the All Black selectors, the trial was a chance to evaluate the strengths and weaknesses of various players in positions (the prop forwards) they were having difficulty in filling. For me, there were the stories involving Chris Laidlaw, Sid Going and Ken Gray's likely successor, as well as the pre-game anti-apartheid protester. All of these personalised the trial for me.

The insights of Saul Alinsky in his book *Rules for*

Radicals are useful, too, in establishing what the personal narratives are in this context. Alinsky argued that events (like rugby matches, presumably) become experience only after they have been reflected on. For most people, life is a series of happenings that go through their system 'undigested'. The happenings are not internalised, in other words. Happenings become experience (or what I call narratives) when they are digested. The digested happenings, which have been turned into part of a person's existence, or experience, can then be related to general patterns and synthesised.

The good watcher of rugby, following Alinsky's paradigm, opens himself or herself up to a plethora of narratives by knowing as much as possible about rugby, its history, its laws, its culture, its tribalism, its literature, its beauty, its ugliness, its customs, the players and the thinkers, what happened in past games and what might happen in the future.

They know, or should know, what the advantages or disadvantages are playing with the wind, whether it is best to have the captain in the forwards, whether one of the centres should be a tackler and the other a runner, how tall the loosehead prop should be, and so on – in short, the zen of rugby, which embraces the thousands of bits of information needed to understand rugby practice and culture.

The good watcher, too, will always try to be at the game. Certainly you can 'watch' rugby on television, or imagine the game through a radio commentary, but these methods are one step removed, like viewing a print of a painting, rather than the painting itself.

If you are not at the game, you miss the big-picture view. The television screen gives close-ups of individual contests but it can show only one event at a time – a scrum, say, or a maul, or a big tackle.

This, moreover, is the view the television commentator gets. Commentators must talk only about what appears on the television monitor in front of them. They are at the ground, but they see only what a person at home in front of their television set sees. And the screen can't show you where all the players are, nor all the contests and events that occur at any one time during a match.

If you go into the studios where the television commentators do their broadcasts at the major rugby grounds, you will see a small screen placed below their eye level so they can see the field and the screen. What will surprise the onlooker who may be allowed to stand silently at the back of the box during the match broadcast is that the commentators and the men who provide the colour, the Gordon Brays and Murray Mexteds, look down to the screen, rather than across to the field. In other words they, too, see the match through the pictures selected by the producers.

One time when I was in a commentary box as an observer for a test, there were roars from the crowd which weren't reflected in the dull passage of play on the field. The commentator turned back to me and mouthed, 'What's happening out there?' The irony was exquisite. Here was a commentator seemingly describing test-match action to hundreds of thousands of watchers around the world, and he had to ask someone what was going on. I quickly wrote a note: 'A couple of players were having a scuffle well away from the play.'

The live 'seeing-in' experience is best because the good watcher can control what he or she wants to see at the game. With the advent of the big screen at the main stadiums, the watcher can also get the close-ups, while still being able to put the scrum or the maul or the line-out that is being highlighted into the context of what is happening around the field. By comparison, if you watch a match on television, you are dependent on the pictures the producer allows you to see. You see the director's game.

With the 'seeing-in' theory now under control, it's time to emulate Captain Cook and take a voyage around the world of rugby. Andre Maurois, the French writer, said that 'you get out of reading exactly what you put into it'. The same discipline applies for watching rugby.

'Rugby, of course, is the perfect game. All the necessary elements are there. It is exceptionally difficult to play well, and to make a move work extraordinary precision and control are needed in the most hostile of British sports journalist Adam Nicholson *circumstances. But at the same time – at the moment that finesse has to be put into action – it demands a boxer's depth of resolution in the service of the skills of a watchmaker.'*

Skills of a
watchmaker

I WAS FIRST introduced to rugby, the perfect game, at the age of five at the convent school, Star of the Sea, Seatoun, Wellington. I couldn't speak a word of English when I was deposited by my parents at the front gate of the school. Perhaps part of the attraction of rugby was my feeling that playing the New Zealand game would make me accepted as a dinkum Kiwi.

I watched my first test on 3 September 1949, when the All Blacks lost to the Wallabies 11–6 at Wellington's Athletic Park. This was perhaps the blackest day in New Zealand rugby history: on the same day the frontline All

Black squad (without any Maori players, who had been prevented from going by the apartheid policies of the South African government) lost to the Springboks at Durban 9–3.

I saw the All Blacks win for the first time at Athletic Park a year later, against the British Lions. I sat on the western bank, a sharply sloping hill oozing mud. I was jammed in with thousands of other spectators, all of us huddling together trying to shelter from a biting wind and slanting showers of rain. Around the time for the test to start, I got an uncontrollable urge to urinate. But going to the toilet meant giving up my excellent position towards the top of the bank opposite the halfway mark of the field. This is the best place to watch rugby, and I had got it only by arriving at the ground in the early hours of the morning. There was nothing for it. I surreptitiously unbuttoned my trouser's fly and released a gentle, controlled flow of urine on to the gabardine overcoat of the unsuspecting Scots College boy sitting in front of me.

This test has remained in my memory. Some people mark the significant moments in their lives by a particular song. I mark the passages of my life with the memories of great rugby teams, players and matches I have watched. And from this treasure house of personal memories I have come to understand that there is a moral ethic in rugby that, if it is embraced by the dedicated watchers of the game, enhances the way they live their lives.

When I taught at St Patrick's College, Silverstream, I was told that 'a good rugby school is a good school'. This assertion that there is a moral dimension to rugby is not as banal as it seems. Rugby is a manly game. You play for your team. You take your knocks, give as hard as you receive, but you do not do anything underhand. You don't pass to someone in a worse position than yourself. You take the tackle yourself, if necessary. You play the ball, not the man.

The erratic bounce of the ball gives rugby an anarchical aspect. You never know precisely what will happen next. The round ball in soccer, for instance, has an inevitability about the way it rolls, thereby reducing the element of luck and unpredictability in the game. But no rugby movement is exactly the same because of the contrariness of the ball, which scuttles and wheels like a tiny terrier doing somersaults. This contrariness mirrors the contrariness of life. Rugby teaches you to accept life's bounce of the ball. The rugby watcher learns to take the bad and the unfair with the good and the fair. A rugby match intensifies the emotions in a 'crowded hour of glorious life'. It is a heightened reality. Winning is important. But accepting defeat graciously is also (or should be) the mark of a rugby supporter.

For some people, these values are as limited as the lines that mark out the rugby paddock. But, simple though they are, I believe they have an integrity and honesty about them, and that generations of rugby players and rugby watchers trying to live by these principles have contributed to the generally decent nature of our society. As Denis Welch once pointed out in an editorial in the *New Zealand Listener*: 'Rugby remains one of the great games, perhaps precisely because it totally involves the body, not just the feet, or a stick or a racquet. Is there any sporting thrill in the world to equal that of a great try? There are also qualities about the sport, qualities like unselfishness and unpretentiousness, that distinguish it from flashier rivals.'

I had worked as editorial writer on the *Sydney Morning Herald* for about 20 years when I learnt that the newspaper's rugby columnist Evan Whitton, a brilliant and controversial analyst, was about to retire. I rushed to the office of the then editor, John Alexander. 'I want to take over Evan Whitton's column,' I told him.

Unperturbed by my aggressive approach, Alexander responded coolly, 'What do you know about rugby?'

'I'm a New Zealander. New Zealanders know everything about rugby,' I replied.

I got the job, which required me to watch and write about all the important rugby matches, and lived happily ever after.

Knowing everything about rugby is a mark of New Zealanders of a certain age. Touring teams used to marvel at the way, for instance, the chambermaids cleaning up their rooms could give the players a dissertation with a PhD degree of difficulty on why their backline wasn't functioning properly, or why their scrum was buckling because the feet alignment of the tight-head prop was all wrong. (In rugby law, the ball must be put into the middle of the scrum by the halfback. 'Middle' is measured as equidistant from the feet of the opposing props. A clever prop like Ken Gray can move the 'middle' of the scrum towards his own side by planting his feet as far back as possible.)

Playing and watching rugby was our religion. The grounds where we watched the tests were our cathedrals. The paddocks where we watched our local teams play were our chapels. The best players were our saints and the opposition thugs were our sinners. Referees who gave penalties against our sides were devils. The cry of 'Black! Black! Black!' emanating from the stands and terraces in great roars of sound was New Zealand's prayer. We knew the hagiographical stories of all the great players: how Bert Cooke, the tiny, electrifying centre of the 1920s, a player of genius, put beer bottles in his coat pockets to bump up his weight to about 60 kilo-grams; how Fergie McCormick never missed a tackle and never had a birthday after his twenty-ninth. From the thousands of accounts gleaned from memory, newspaper columns, books on rugby and, more recently, television interviews, we knew hundreds of personal stories.

I call both these hagiographical stories and the personal stories 'narratives'. They have been created for over 100 years now by generations of watchers of rugby, and are the catechism of the rugby religion. For many generations, they have also defined what being a New Zealander is. But no longer, perhaps. I have the feeling that the claim that 'New Zealanders know everything about rugby' cannot be sustained. Kids don't have to play rugby as they did when I was a youngster. Other sports and other interests have grabbed the attention of the younger generations. The rugby tests still generate great interest. But they don't hold the nation in their thrall as, say, the tour of the 1956 Springboks did. Warwick Roger's splendid book on that tour, *Old Heroes*, worthy of a top five place in any list of great rugby books, sums up this loss of a rugby-watching hegemony in its title.

And there has been the nonsense peddled by experts who should know better that there is something wrong with being a watcher. Not enough people participate, the argument runs. We are becoming a nation of watchers. This is said to be a bad thing. The same sort of people who make this argument complain, as well, that not enough people read books. But what is the real difference between reading a book and watching a rugby match? Nothing, essentially. Reading and watching rugby are positive activities. They are not passive activities like having a shower – where a tap does all the work. The reader and the rugby watcher are doing something. Their activity enhances what the author has written or what the players achieve on the field. They 'take in' what is happening on the page or on the field.

They turn their take into a personal experience that enriches their lives.

No reader reads a book in the same way as all the other readers. Similarly, the watchers of a rugby match 'read' the play differently from other watchers depending on the narratives they bring to the game. I would argue that, because of rather than despite these different experiences, New Zealanders have lost something wonderfully enhancing to their lives, and to the nation's cultural and spiritual well-being, with the loss of a rugby-watching hegemony.

A revival of the old-time religion of watching rugby is needed.

'At its best, rugby is a game that all the gods of Greece might crowd the northern skies to see, and, benched on our cold clouds, be not restrained either by frozen bottoms or the crowd's chill sceptic hearts from plunging to the aid of the stronger Myrmidons, of plucking from the scrummage some Hector trodden in the mire and nursing him to strength again. Well might the Thunderer send fleet Mercury, swooping from the heights, to pick from the empty air Achilles' mis-flung pass and with it race — dog-rose and buttercup fast springing in his track — to the eternal goal.'

Eric Linklater,
Scottish poet,
novelist and
historian

The Greeks invented football

THE ANCIENT GREEKS had a game called *episkyros* that had many similarities to modern rugby. Vases dug up from ancient sites reveal depictions of scantily clad males in ballet-exercise type poses with languid, outstretched arms, playing with a round ball. Centuries later, around 1600, the Welsh played a similar sort of football game called *cnapan*. The game was as hard to play as its name was to pronounce. It seems to have been an early version of coarse rugby, the game played in obscure grounds mainly for the socialising that takes place afterwards. Cnapan players did not wear uniforms or boots. They were naked. The object of their endeavours was to hurl, push, kick or in any way force the cnapan, a round wooden ball that had been boiled in fat to make it slippery, between one village and another.

Variations of this form of football (to give the exercise a generic name) were common, though, to most societies throughout the ages. The Romans, borrowing as usual from the Greeks, called their game *harpastum*. This Roman game seemed to have more muscularity in it than the Greek game. According to *The World of Rugby*, an excellent history written for the BBC by noted rugby journalist John Reason and distinguished coach Carwyn James, 'The game was started by throwing the ball into the air between the two teams, who then tried to carry it forward to lines marked at each end of the field of play. To do this they had to maul for possession of the ball, they had to support each other to drive it forward, which is the essence of the modern scrummage, and they had to pass it.' It is clear from this description that the elements of modern rugby – the mauling, scrumming and passing tactics, played on a field with marked dimensions – were inherent in the Greco-Roman form of football.

Medieval English soldiers, wearing their armour (unlike the naked Welsh cnapan footballers), liked to celebrate their victories by kicking the heads of their slain opponents around the battlefield. Edward II banned this form of football in London in 1314. Perhaps he thought his head might one day be booted around some field.

The rugby game as we know it today, though, was invented in the public schools of England. The game and its code of behaviour were spread with zeal by public school old boys throughout the British colonies in the late nineteenth century. The game was seen as the perfect foundry to create the manly, brave and pugnacious men needed to rule an Empire on which the sun never set.

'Maybe if we didn't have sport we'd be going to war even more often than we do. It's a safe version – or comparatively so – of something more serious. It does seem to be written deep in our genetic disposition, even if its discontents have been around as long as sport itself. Socrates, for instance, incurred the displeasure of ancient Athens for not taking the hoplite (weaponry and tactics) training seriously enough … Human stories, which, like sport, are fake – safe, exaggerated versions of something more real and serious. The evidence seems to be that we need these diversions. They're stories, recreation – play – and all animals, not just humans, use play to develop living skills, to learn about life.'

Alan Close,
Good Weekend,
Sydney
Morning
Herald

Going to war

THE TERMINOLOGY of rugby as it evolved out of English public schools in the nineteenth century was intimately connected with the ethic of warfare. Understand that rugby is a war game and you understand the zen of rugby. Lord Jellicoe, First Sea Lord during the First World War, expressed the connection this way: 'Rugby football, to my mind, above all games is one which develops the qualities which go to make good fighting men. It teaches unselfishness, esprit de corps, quickness of decision, and keeps fit all those engaged in it.'

The terminology of rugby is steeped in war rhetoric.

Rugby people talk about 'bombs', those high, steepling kicks with attackers racing through, which test the fortitude and courage of the catcher. There are chip kicks 'over the top', a reference to soldiers leaving their trenches in the front line to attack their opponents. Players fire off 'torpedo' kicks. Attacks are mounted down the 'flanks', the extremities of the field. 'Offensive defence' is espoused as the best way to disrupt the other team. Attacks are 'launched', as if they are battleships. Defences are 'blown away', as if hand grenades have been thrown at them. Halfbacks 'snipe' around the blindside. Loose forwards are 'marauders'. Teams that have adventurous runners are said to have 'strike power'. Forwards and sometimes backs 'kill' the ball in rucks and mauls. Line-outs and scrums are 'won' against the throw or the head. A ferocious tackle is admiringly described as a 'big hit'. A snappy passing halfback is said to have a 'bullet' pass.

The famous three Ps – Possession, Position, Pace – of the 1938 All Black Charlie Saxton could stand as short-hand for the principles espoused by a great military strategist. Players are said to put 'their bodies on the line'. Murray Mexted, a former All Black and now a colourful rugby commentator, came out with this memorable remark as the All Blacks defeated the Wallabies at Eden Park in 2003 to win back the Bledisloe Cup: 'Well, it's like a war. To the victor goes the spoils and the spoils are a huge trophy, huge competition, huge rivalry between two countries, huge respect …' When England won the 2003 World Cup, the victory was called by an enthusiastic journalist, 'England's greatest win outside of the two World Wars.'

But the war analogy should not be carried too far. Rugby is a war game. It is not actual warfare. As Murray Mexted says, 'It's like a war.' Rugby is a 'safe version' of war, as Alan Close argues. Nor should rugby be singled out by sports historians, as it is too often, as the war game of all the sports. The Australian playwright David Williamson makes the point about Australian Rules Football that 'it's about war fought within rules'. And this is true of rugby, as well. War is such an extreme experience, its terror and awfulness are undervalued if the analogy of rugby or any other sport as a war game is carried too far.

But using the war game metaphor can help the good watcher understand rugby strategy and the tactics used by teams to win a match. For example, at the 1999 World Cup the Wallaby coach, Rod Macqueen, insisted that his preparations for his team were greatly influenced by the teachings of the ancient Chinese warrior-philosopher Sun-tzu. One of the dictums from Sun-tzu's *The Art of War* had a special resonance with Macqueen: 'In planning, never a useless move, in strategy, no steps taken in vain.' It was no accident that the Wallabies always seemed to be one move ahead of their opponents throughout the tournament.

'I once dated a famous Aussie rugby player who treated me just like a football: he made a pass, played footsie, then dropped me as soon as he scored.'

Author Kathy Lette, quoted on a BBC Sports website

Making a pass

I WAS WATCHING THE ACT Brumbies playing the Auckland Blues early in the 2003 Super 12 season on my television at home when I experienced a ruck 'n' roll moment. I had the earphones plugged into the television set so that my wife, who was making dinner in the kitchen, could listen to classical music on the radio. Wet and slippery conditions were making things difficult for the players. An even contest was finally blown wide open for the Blues when the Fijian winger, Rupeni Caucaunibuca, a player built along the comfortable lines of a well-fed banker but incredibly fast, scored a sensational try.

The ball squirted from a ruck near the sideline. Caucaunibuca swooped on it.

'Oh! Oh!' I exclaimed, quite loudly because of the din coming through my headphones. Caucaunibuca stepped inside one of the Brumbies defenders. 'Oh! Oh! Oh!' I exclaimed again. Caucaunibuca ran around George Gregan, one of the great defenders. 'Oh! Oh! Oh! Oh!' I exclaimed. Then Caucaunibuca raced through the cover defence, and with a huge grin on his face planted the ball under the posts.

'Oh! Oh! Oh! O my god! O my god!' I yelled out.

My wife called out, finally, from the kitchen: 'Are you having an orgasm out there?'

'I am in a way,' I replied.

Sports historians would suggest that my sexual frisson is not a rare thing for the rugby watcher, or player. The historians point out that during the 1870s up to about 1900 — the first 30 years rugby was played in New Zealand — there was an oversupply of men to women. The gender numbers did not come into balance until the 1900s. According to Jock Phillips in his pioneering study of New Zealand male culture, *A Man's Country*, before then there was a widespread belief that 'rugby helped sublimate sexuality and provided a healthy alternative to bad habits, particularly masturbation'.

Phillips argues that there is some merit in this belief. Until the Second World War, he claims, many New Zealand males did not get married until their late twenties, and even then the restrictions on their sex life were considerable. 'It is not inconceivable that playing rugby helped to sublimate acute sexual frustration ... It may have given males a form of physical contact which they could not legitimately get elsewhere,' he concludes.

The linkage between what goes on in the rucks and mauls and what may go on between the sheets has been memorably made by Lisa Wilkinson, the wife of the bear-like (that is, big enough to play in the second row for the Wallabies) sports writer Peter FitzSimons: 'I can remember as a teenager watching Wallaby test matches on TV and looking at those rucks and mauls, and thinking, I wonder what it would be like to be buried beneath all those hot, sweaty, greasy mounds of rutted rugby flesh, gasping for air, being forced to do things against your will? And now, after ten years of sharing a bed with Pete, I think, Ah well, maybe I know.'

If the Phillips' thesis is right, the mating call of the rugby male watcher may well have been summarised by a campaign slogan promoted during the 2003 World Cup by a Sydney brothel, Stiletto. The brothel hired a truck that made its way through the CBD streets bearing the words: 'Fancy a ruck? ... Knock-on tonight at Stiletto.'

'In America, a guy might wake his partner up in the middle of the night to make love. The Kiwi bloke would wake her up to watch the All Blacks on TV.'

The Daily Telegraph (UK)

Consensual rugby

FOR NEW ZEALAND men, as the supercilious *Daily Telegraph* suggests, there is never a contest when it comes to deciding whether to watch a test match in bed or have sex. The pleasure of rugby rucks apparently prevails over the pleasure of sexual rucking. Or so we are told. Keith Quinn, the veteran rugby broadcaster, who dug up this quotation, added the gloss that 'any sensible Kiwi bloke would wake his partner in the middle of the night and get her to organise the tea and the biscuits so she could watch the game with him'.

If the partner is smart, she will go along with the request. During the 2003 Rugby World Cup, BBC Sport ran an interview with a sex therapist, Jo-Anne Baker, who stressed that the worst thing a 'rugby widow' could do was to make her partner choose between rugby and sex. Baker was quoted as saying: 'It's not about saying it's an either-or. It's about saying we can have both.'

Baker then went on to reveal that a woman's best chance of getting intimate with her partner was if his team won. 'Guys can celebrate the win of their favourite team by having great sex,' she insisted.

The same game plan presumably applies to players, but for them, there is a more elemental issue: does sex before rugby help or hinder their performance on the field?

During the 2003 World Cup the Springboks were banned from having any sex for the entire tournament. The opposite was offered to the Fijians. Fiji's Air Pacific introduced special 'love fares' for the wives and girl-friends of the players. The boss of Fijian rugby endorsed the special treatment. 'Having the company of women you love is certainly part of the happy-making process,' he told reporters. 'It has always been my experience that a happy player is a successful player.' The wives and partners of the Wallabies were able to spend time with the players at their training headquarters but were kept apart in the days leading up to the final matches. The All Blacks followed the same regime.

The French, however, worked on an incentive plan. If France made the semi-finals, the wives and girlfriends of the players could move into their hotel. France's five-eighth, Frederic Michalak, gave journalists the drill. 'We're here,' he said in an interview, 'for big victories, not big breasts.' England allowed the partners of players to stay with them throughout the tour, if they wanted. Jonny Wilkinson's girlfriend stayed in England.

Fiji under-performed on the field. France made the semi-finals and then played a tame, distracted match against England and an even more lacklustre and limp performance against New Zealand to lose the third-place play-off. This was after their wives and girlfriends had moved into their hotel. The Springboks were without power or drive in their quarter-final loss to the All Blacks. The Wallabies played their best matches at the end of the tournament, defeating the All Blacks convincingly and then being equal with England into the last 28 seconds of extra time. And England, the team with the most balanced approach to the issue of 'to bed or not to bed', won the tournament with consistently strong and virile play.

This outcome seems to support the views of Roman historian Pliny the Elder (77 AD), who claimed: 'Athletes, when sluggish, are revitalised by love-making.'

The legendary baseball coach Casey Stengel gave a memorable, and probably the most credible, answer to the sex-before-the-match issue: 'The trouble is not that players have sex the night before a game; it's that they stay out all night looking for it.'

'No other game permits men to plough opponents into the ground and then cheerfully help them to their feet to suffer like treatment in reverse. For boys, rugby is the game for the sunshine of their lives, when the world is full and round and there is health and wonder in the air: a game of the mind as well as the body, and a test and source of character. Rugby football inspires all those qualities of skill and courage, magnanimity, cooperation and unselfishness that give the game its universal appeal to men of free spirit.'

Anonymous citation sent to the *Sydney Morning Herald* by a letter writer in 1995

A short history of nearly everything about rugby

, 1823 RUNNING WITH THE ball is allegedly introduced into the game of football at Rugby School in England. This is the origin of the myth of William Webb Ellis, concocted by Rugbeians in 1895.

1841 Running with the ball is officially allowed in Rugby School's rules, provided the ball is taken on the bounce. Passing is specifically forbidden. Over the decades many rugby commentators from the southern hemisphere have argued that British rugby has continued to maintain this rule.

1857 *Tom Brown's Schooldays* by Thomas Hughes is published. This book is read by tens of thousands of youngsters, and immortalises the culture and language of rugby as practised by the boys at Rugby School. One of those youngsters is Baron Pierre de Coubertin, the founder of the modern Olympic movement. Coubertin is taken with the English notions of manly gamesmanship propounded in the cult novel. He believes these notions are among the highest expressions of the human spirit. Because of his influence, rugby is introduced into the Olympic Games in 1908, with Australia winning the first gold medal. The United States wins the Olympic gold medal for rugby in 1912 and 1920.

1862 The indiarubber bladder for the rugby ball is invented. This is the essential technological advance in rugby equipment. The original pigskin bladders had been so disgusting to blow that boys at Rugby School left this odious task to Mr Gilbert, a nearby boot maker. Gilbert's family subsequently developed a worldwide business in providing rugby balls. The balls used in the 2003 Rugby World Cup tournament carry the Gilbert brand name.

Pigskin bladders had many other disadvantages, too. They lost their shape and disintegrated quite quickly when subjected to relentless kicking. The indiarubber bladders solved all these problems. Encased in tough leather, they produced a rugby ball that resisted indefinitely the impact of the elements and multitudinous kicks.

With the new mass-produced ball, rugby is ready to

move out of the cloisters of a handful of English public schools into the bigger community of young men in the colonies.

1863 The Rugby Football Union (the self-styled England Rugby Union) is formed and a meeting is held in London to draw up a standard set of laws. The laws of the Rugby Union are written to differ from the Association Football (soccer) laws in their allowance of the use of hands in catching and passing the ball. Goals, successful kicks over a post, rather than under the post as in soccer, are taken after a team scores a try. The try enables the successful side to 'try' to kick a goal. Charging, tripping and hacking are allowed. Hacking is the action of repeatedly kicking at the ball trapped in the maul of players. It often causes serious injuries to shinbones, knees and other parts of players caught in the pile-up.

Rugby is seen as a dribbling game rather than a handling/running/kicking game.

1865 On 21 August the *Sydney Morning Herald* runs an account of the first rugby match played in the southern hemisphere: 'Football. A match was commenced on Saturday afternoon, on the University ground, between players of the University and the Sydney Club. After an exciting struggle, which lasted about an hour and a half, during which no goal was obtained, the match was drawn, owing to a misunderstanding regarding the rules …'

1869 The first football game under rugby rules is played in the United States, between Rutgers and Princeton.

1870 The Wellington (New Zealand) Club is formed and the first inter-provincial match is played in Petone, against the Nelson Club, under Rugby School rules provided by C. J. Munro.

1871 The first president of the Rugby Football Union, A. Rutter, and two other Rugbeians, E. C. Holmes and L. T. Maton, draft the new laws based on the 1863 rules for the 'union' game. They adopt the most recent laws of Rugby School, except for a couple of changes in kicking requirements.

The first international rugby match, between England and Scotland, is played. There are 20 players a side: 13 forwards, three halfbacks, one three-quarter and three fullbacks. Richard Lindon, a resident of the town of Rugby, makes the indiarubber bladder for a match ball. He makes the shape of the bladder distinctly plum-shaped to fit in with the shape of the ball required for the Rugby School game, in which the ball has to be kicked over, rather than through, the crossbar.

1870 Oxford and Cambridge reduce their teams to 15 players.

1870 Wellington College (14) and Nelson College (0) meet at the Basin Reserve in the first inter-college rugby match in New Zealand. This was probably the first inter-college match played anywhere in the world. The first inter-school match in England did not take place until 1896, when Rugby (0) lost to Cheltenham (13).

1877 Hacking is abolished. This gives rise to Law 47: 'No hacking, or hacking over, or tripping up shall be allowed under any circumstances. No one wearing projecting nails, iron plates or gutta perch on any part of his boots or shoes will be allowed to play in a match.' The *Bulletin* calls rugby 'the undertaker's friend', despite the reform.

Player numbers in international matches are reduced from 20 to 15.

1881 Alan Rotherman, a halfback at Oxford University, develops passing to his outside backs. Wales adopts a team formation in line with this development: nine forwards, two halfbacks, two three-quarters and two fullbacks.

1882 New South Wales, with a squad of only 15 players, tours New Zealand. The team plays seven games, winning four and losing three.

Neutral referees are appointed for international matches for the first time.

1884 The first New Zealand representative side visits Australia and wins all eight matches.

The use of the whistle by referees becomes accepted practice in New Zealand.

1886 A numerical value is adopted by the Rugby Football Union in England for tries and goals (successful conversions of tries), with three tries made equal to one goal. This reform uses the scoring system at Cheltenham College, which gives a points value to a try, unlike the Rugby School scoring system.

1888 The England rugby team visits Australia and New Zealand, introducing locals to the concept of heeling from scrummages and the systematic passing game. It wins 13, draws four, loses two.

A New Zealand 'Natives' team makes a return visit, touring New Zealand, Australia and Great Britain. The team plays 74 matches, winning 49 (including a defeat of Ireland), losing 20 (including defeats by Wales and England) and drawing five.

1890 The International Rugby Board (IRB) is formed to settle disputes and make laws governing international fixtures. The board has twelve members: six representing England; two each from Scotland, Wales and Ireland. The so-called Home Unions still dominate the IRB, unfortunately.

1893 J. P. Firth, later to become a long-serving headmaster of Wellington College, gives a try to a player from the Athletic Club after he has been impeded in his chase for the ball. This 'penalty' try is contested by the opposition, East Christchurch. The argument goes to the IRB to be resolved. Firth's reasoning wins the day.

In terms of the development of the laws of rugby, the penalty try ruling and its theoretical justification on the basis that teams should be allowed to convert an 'advantage' into points if the opposition commits a breach of the laws, is as important as the development of the indiarubber bladder. It means that the laws of the game are flexible and able to be improved.

Cardiff creates a formation of eight forwards and seven backs. This is so successful it is universally adopted.

1895 The coal-mining northern counties of Yorkshire and Lancashire are kicked out of the England Football Union for demanding that players be paid for time off work. This initiates the Great Split between amateur rugby union and professional rugby league.

Referees are given sole charge of matches, with their decisions regarded as final.

A group of Rugby School old boys sets up a commission to establish the 'fact' that William Webb Ellis picked up the ball and ran with it in a match on the Big Field in 1823. The committee cajoles Thomas Hughes, the author of *Tom Brown's Schooldays*, to confirm the Ellis story. Hughes refuses to cooperate. The change to running forward at Rugby School came in 1834 not 1823, he insisted: 'And indeed became rather popular in 1838/39 from the prowess of Jem Mackie, the great runner-in.'

The creation of the William Webb Ellis myth, and the ejection of the coal-mining counties, entrenches an exclusionist ethic in British rugby (except for Wales) and, because the Home Unions dominate its official positions, the International Rugby Board.

The 'old farts' — former England captain Will Carling's term of derision — of British rugby made their last stand against adopting the inclusive ethic when the England, Ireland and Scotland unions voted against holding a Rugby World Cup tournament in 1987. Wales split its vote. The born-to-rule rugby illusion was maintained, though, with the insistence of the Home Unions that the trophy for the tournament be named after the icon of the exclusionist ethic, William Webb Ellis.

1903 The first test is played by a New Zealand representative side (22) against Australia (3) at the Sydney Cricket Ground.

1905 The All Blacks defeat England 15–0 at Crystal Palace, London. The official crowd is 45,000 but estimates have gone as high as 70,000. This is the biggest crowd for a football match in England. The All Blacks, with their 'all backs' game, with the forwards hunting as a pack of hounds, with their decoy moves and team organisation, revolutionise rugby and create the modern game.

Bouncing the ball into the line-out is abolished: the

ball has to be thrown in. Scoring of three points for a try, five points for a converted try and three for a penalty is universally adopted.

1907 Dally Messenger, the David Campese of his day, is lured across to the professional code of rugby league by a group of Sydney entrepreneurs.

1908 The Australian Wallabies win the gold medal for rugby at the London Olympic Games, defeating the England county champions Cornwall, the only other entrant.

1909 Rugby league becomes the major football code in New South Wales and Queensland after the purchase by Sydney entrepreneur Joynton Smith of most of the 1908 Olympic gold medal-winning Wallaby side. This poaching tactic has similarities with the Super League takeover bid almost 90 years later. A strong rugby league presence is established in Auckland.

1914 The IRB bans paid coaches and trainers from any level of rugby.

1919 'Mother Country' (with only one non-officer in the team), New Zealand (one officer only), Australia (three officers), South Africa and Canada play an Empire Inter-Services Tournament – the first rugby 'World Cup'. New Zealand defeats the 'Mother Country' in the final at Twickenham.

1924/25 The 'Invincibles' New Zealand team wins every match of its tour of Britain, France and British Columbia. George Nepia, the 19-year-old Maori fullback, plays every match and becomes rugby's first international superstar.

1926 The IRB decides that each of the two halves in an international match should be of 40 minutes' duration.

1937 South Africa wins the test series in New Zealand for the first time and is dubbed 'the greatest team ever to leave New Zealand'. This is the first test series lost by the All Blacks in New Zealand.

The IRB rules that conversions for penalty tries must be taken in front of the goalposts. The laws involving the tackle, scrummage and penalty kicks are substantially changed.

1948 New Zealand and Australia are admitted to the IRB.

1956 New Zealand defeats South Africa in a test series for the first time. This is the first series loss by the Springboks in the twentieth century.

1958 A significant change is made in the tackle ball law: players, after regaining their feet, are permitted to play the ball after a tackle in any lawful way (rather than only with their feet).

1968 Replacements for injured players are allowed in tests.

1971 Revolutionary law changes are introduced to devalue the kicking game: players are required to stand behind the hindmost foot in the scrum; backs, except the halfback, are to stand ten metres from the line-out; no kicks directly into touch are allowed from outside the 22-metre line; a try is upgraded to four points.

1972 The first direct telecast by satellite of a test match – New Zealand (19), Wales (16) – takes place at Cardiff.

1981 The Gilbert Company introduces a range of synthetic balls based on technological innovations in design, manufacture and materials.

1987 New Zealand wins the first Rugby World Cup, a 16-team invitational tournament co-hosted by the New Zealand Rugby Union and the Australian Rugby Union.

1991 Australia wins the second Rugby World Cup, defeating England in the final at Twickenham 12–3. Towards the end of the final, with the Wallaby backs reluctant to boot the ball downfield, their agitated coach, Bob Dwyer, yells out: 'Kick it to the shit house!' The upper lip of the Queen, who is sitting two rows in front of Dwyer, does not twitch.

The United States wins the inaugural Women's Rugby World Cup, defeating England 19–6.

1993 The five-point try is introduced. This is the deci-
sive change in the scoring system. For the first time, two
tries are worth more points than three penalties or drop
goals. The change confirms that, theoretically at least,
rugby is a game of try-scoring rather than penalty-scoring.

1995 The Springboks, playing in their first Rugby
World Cup, defeat the 'poisoned' All Blacks in a final that
goes into overtime. Nelson Mandela virtually wins the
match for the home side when he wears a Springbok jersey
as he shakes hands with both teams before the match.

Under mounting pressure from a rugby league Super
League, the IRB decides that 'rugby is no longer an amateur game'. Players are officially offered contracts and the
brave new world of professional rugby union begins. The
reform comes 100 years after the fateful decision to outlaw
professionalism.

1996 The inaugural Super 12 and Tri-Nations tournaments begin.

1999 The Wallabies defeat the All Blacks at the
Olympic Stadium in Sydney before a world-record crowd
of 107,042 spectators.

Australia wins its second Rugby World Cup. Once again
it is an away win. The favourites, the All Blacks, succumb
weakly in the second half of their semi-final with France.
The New Zealand coach, John Hart, is blamed for the
defeat. The nation goes into a deep depression.

2003 A hundred years after the first rugby test between New Zealand and Australia, the All Blacks defeat the Wallabies at Eden Park. The All Blacks win back the Bledisloe Cup, donated by Lord Bledisloe in 1931, for the first time in five years. Australia's longest stretch of holding the Bledisloe Cup is ended. New Zealand's longest winning run is from 1951 to 1979.

In one of the greatest rugby matches ever played, the Rugby World Cup is won by England in a dramatic match against Australia that goes into overtime and is finally won 28 seconds from time when Jonny Wilkinson drop-kicks a fateful goal.

2005 Wales, under captain Gareth Thomas, defeats Ireland 32-20 to win the Six Nations European rugby tournament with a Grand Slam of victories. The cele-brations are attended by Prince Charles (Prince of Wales) and the Duchess of Cornwall (the former Camilla Parker-Bowles) on their first official visit to Wales as a married couple. The tournament, which began in 1882 when England played Wales at Swansea, is said to be the world's oldest. It became known as the Five Nations when France officially joined in 1910, and has been played every year since, except the two world wars and 1972 when Scotland and Wales refused to play in Ireland because of its political troubles. Italy joined in 2000.

The Lions tour New Zealand for the first time since 1993. They play 11 matches, including three tests against the All Blacks.

'I watched the All Blacks'
match on television on
Saturday and discovered
that the players in the
scrum in the front are
forwards, and those
standing out behind them
are backs. This is so
bleedingly, forehead-
thumpingly obvious that
I can't believe it took all
Columnist *my life till Saturday night*
Joanne Black, *for the blinding flash to*
Dominion Post *illuminate it. The forwards*
are at the front, the
backs are behind them.
I went to bed on Saturday
night thinking, "The
forwards are at the front,
the backs ..." Life's big
revelations are like that.'

Revelations

ORWARDS IN RUGBY, as Joanne Black discovered, play *on* the ball. Backs generally play *off* the ball. In theory, the forwards win the ball by working as a *pack* and the backs score tries by working together as a *backline*.

The positions in the forwards are designated from where the players are placed in the scrum. The front row is made of two props with a hooker in the middle. The second row consists of four players, two second-rowers (or locks as they are called in New Zealand) and two breakaways. The back row consists of one player, called a lock in Australia or the number 8, which is the number on the back of his jersey, in New Zealand.

The backs are designated from the order in which they line up when a scrum is put down. The halfback (the player who stands halfway between the props in the front row and the fullback) snaps at the heels of the pack. Outside the halfback is the five-eighths (a New Zealand terminology based on the fraction between a half and the three-quarters) or the fly half. Outside the fly half are two centres (or a second five-eighths and a centre in the New Zealand terminology). Outside the centres are the left and right wing three-quarters. And behind this backline is the fullback.

The terms for the various positions are basically self-explanatory. The props actually prop up the scrum. The hooker hooks the ball back from the scrum. But when we get to other terms used in rugby we venture into the arcane world of English public school slang. Trying to explain some of these terms to his American readers of the *International Herald Tribune*, Bob Donahue took this line: 'Touch is the sideline. Ruck, maul, scrum, punt, hack, chip, pass, goal, most of rugby's one-syllable schoolboy words, are Greek to American football fans.'

And American football fans are not the only supporters who have been bewildered. When the laws of rugby were translated into Chinese, the experts found that many of the terms did not make sense. 'In touch', for instance, describes the state of the ball when it is actually out of touch and cannot be played. In the 'dead ball' area, the section of the field from the try line to the last line on the field, the ball is very much in play. This is where tries are scored and force-downs made to restart play on the 22-metre line.

Incidentally, the Chinese rugby authorities insisted that the 'dead ball' phrase be removed from their translation of the laws, as anything that connotes death brings bad luck in their culture.

In his *Pick Me Up and Run*, an excellent little primer on the game, David O'Neil notes: 'There are four different ways of competing for the ball once a game is in progress. These plays are called scrums (scrummage), line-outs, rucks and mauls.' With this terminology we are back to Ed Donahue's schoolboy slang.

I have not read anything definitive on this, but my guess is that we get the word 'scrum', and the form of the scrum, from the Winchester School rules, which provided for a drawn-out, cruel and attritional form of football. The modern scrum involves two packs of eight forwards, binding together in three rows of three, four and one. The ball is placed (in theory) in the middle of the gap between the front rows (the props and hooker) of each scrum. The packs push or scrum over the ball, trying to get it back to their respective halfbacks. One of the merits of the scrum from a strategic viewpoint is that it concentrates all the forwards in a small part of the field and, in theory, enables the backs to have one-on-one contests between the ball-runner and the tackler. The other merit of the scrum is that it acts as a way of forcing an intense physical contest between the forwards, especially those in the front row.

The line-out is what the term indicates. It has evolved in gridiron into the line of scrimmage. But in rugby the two packs line up side by side and jump for the ball, which is thrown in from the sideline down the middle (in theory) of the two packs.

Line-outs used to be dockyard brawls for possession of the ball. There are about 30 different ways the laws of rugby can be broken from the time a ball is thrown into the line-out until it is cleared by the halfback. In fact, it is often said that there has never been a legal line-out in the history of the game. Some order has been injected into this chaos by the reform of allowing jumpers to be lifted. This has given a spectacular and balletic element to the game, with players being lifted to great heights. Being 'good in the air' has become an essential quality for second-rowers. Their huge leaps rival those of Australian Rules players in their breathtaking and soaring defiance of the laws of gravity.

When the players mill and swarm over the ball on the ground, this is a ruck. If, amid the tangle of bodies, the ball is somehow kept off the ground, this is a maul.

What goes on in these rucks and mauls? Peter FitzSimons, a former Wallaby and a colourful sports-writer, has described the descent into what seems like Dante's Inferno this way: 'In an upright position and pushing against the New Zealanders in the rucks and mauls one sees their feet whirring around, spitting the mud out behind them. Fall into that maelstrom and it feels like you were caught tying your shoelaces when the bulls of Pamplona pass through. Smell? I guess they always smelled pretty normal in a rugby sort of way. Eau de Mud, Sweat and Vaseline. Sounds? Groans and grunts of efforts, exchanges of imprecations as the two front rows hit in the scrum, the sound of flesh hitting flesh at speed, the "oooomph!" as a player fringing the ruck gets hit by an opposition player.'

The good watcher should think of the forwards as the foot soldiers, plodding forward through the machine-gun fire, the mines and the shellfire from the artillery. And the backs should be seen as a combination of fighter planes, zooming in and zooming away after hitting their targets, or bombers letting loose their deadly weapons from on high and then returning to the safety of their home bases.

'The main scheme is to work the ball down the field somehow and deposit it over the line at the other end, and in order to squelch this program each side is allowed to put in a certain amount of assault and battery and do things to its fellow man which, if done elsewhere, would result in fourteen days without option, coupled with some strong remarks from the bench.'

English-American novelist and humorist P. G. Wodehouse explaining rugby

A certain amount of assault

RUGBY, AS PEDANTS like to point out, has laws, not rules. Yet it is, as the great humorist P. G. Wodehouse suggests, a somewhat lawless game. How do we explain this paradox?

A famous apocryphal story provides something of an answer. A young referee is appointed to referee Wales in his first test-match appointment. This is in the heyday of Welsh rugby, when the Red Dragons are famous for their shrewdness in exploiting the laws in their own favour. To calm his nerves on the eve of the test, the referee goes into the bar of the hotel where he and the teams are staying. He becomes aware that a group of thickset and beetle-browed men near him are talking in low voices about how they are going to have a field day with the young referee the next day. He assumes these men are members of the Welsh pack. He makes up his mind that he is not going to be exploited.

The following day, scrutinising the Welsh side as the first scrum goes down, he sees nothing wrong. No law has been broken. He blows his whistle and calls out, 'Penalty against Wales.' As the Welsh retreat, he hears one of them say, 'Better give it away boyos, the ref's on to us.'

The laws of rugby are many and detailed. Perhaps this explains why so many lawyers adore rugby. The field is a movable courtroom. The IRB's book *Rugby: The Laws of the Game Made Easier* is 195 pages long. No fewer than six laws of rugby, some of them running into 14 sub-sections, are needed to establish the requirements before a match can proceed.

It is hardly any wonder that David Campese once confessed that he didn't know all the laws of the game. This didn't stop him from being the top try-scorer in the history of test rugby. The wonderful Welsh winger Gerald Davies once told an interviewer: 'I don't think many players know the laws. For my own part, I never actually read the rule book until late in my life.' Three years after he turned from league to rugby union, Jason Robinson, the electric, broken-field runner for England, revealed that he was still uncertain about the laws of his new code. 'The referee often blows his whistle,' he said, 'and I don't know why. But I know what I'm supposed to do. That's the important thing.'

Only the referee knows the laws of the game. The players don't; most regard the laws of rugby a bit like questions in an examination – only four to be attempted. Players do need 'to know what to do', as Robinson suggests. This formula of knowing what to do, or rather what to look for, applies to the good watcher as well. An accountant understands the restrictions that apply to commercial activities, while the entrepreneur concentrates on the horizon-wide possibilities. The best players, and the best watchers, are rugby entrepreneurs, not accountants.

Rugby is a game for all shapes and sizes. The laws of rugby accept this inclusiveness; the physical democracy of the game is matched by a similar law-democracy which makes rugby a relatively easy game for players who do not know most of the laws. For these players it's like knowing how to turn on a light switch, without having the remotest idea how the electricity is conveyed. In rugby, you only have to know that you play behind the ball, that you don't tackle someone unless he (or increasingly, with the growth of women's rugby, she) has the ball, that tackles should be on the chest and downwards, that passes must not be thrown forward, that you shouldn't dive over the ball in rucks and mauls, that once there is a ruck you have to use your feet (but only on the ball, not on your opponents) to get it back, and that line-out throws and scrum feeds should be 'down the middle'.

Each position, particularly in the forwards, has its own body of knowledge. But this knowledge need be mastered only by the specialist. Backs, for instance, have no idea of what goes on in the front row. The scrum is a dark world of heaving shoulders, clashing heads and hacking boots best left to the battle-scarred veterans of the front row to fight out among themselves. It is the underworld of rugby. If you ask a hooker, for instance, the score of a match, he'll probably tell you that he won two scrums against the head. Dominating the scrums and throwing in accurately is his game.

Rugby has been described as chess played by massive pieces who are allowed to smash into each other. And like chess there are in rugby innumerable permutations and variations of play for which the framework of the laws allows. The laws have to be flexible enough to cover all these variations. There are about 200 events — scrums, kick-off, penalties, line-outs, mauls and rucks — in an 80-minute rugby match. And within these events there are many subsidiary events. Is the ball thrown in straight in the line-out? Are the thrower's feet behind the touch line? Does he throw in without baulking? Do any of the jumpers cross the invisible line down the middle of the line-out? Do the lifters have the correct grip on the shorts of the lifted player? With all these complications it is understandable that the actual laws are a complicated document.

The laws, too, have to be flexible enough to cope with events that cannot be foretold. Every game is different.

Things happen that have never happened before. The laws have to take in events that the lawmakers could never have envisaged. There has been an instance of a hang-glider landing in a ruck. What decision does a referee make with an event of this kind? What about a ball lodging in telegraph lines overhanging the field of play?

The innovative Australian coach Daryl Haberecht made this point: 'The laws of the game tell you what you can't do. Only your imagination limits what you can do.' Haberecht invented the 'up-the-jersey' ploy. He got his team to line up for a penalty with their backs to the opposition. One player stuffed the ball up his jersey. The rest of the team placed their arms up their jerseys. At the signal, all the players turned on their opponents and sprinted towards the try line. The opposition did not know whom to tackle and Greg Cornelsen (who scored a record four tries against the All Blacks at Eden Park in 1978) cantered away for a try.

Another example of inventiveness under pressure is provided by Sir Edward 'Weary' Dunlop, the cranky and immensely brave doctor-hero at Changi, who took beatings and privations to ensure proper treatment of the imprisoned Australian troops. He was a Wallaby in the 1930s. In a test against New Zealand at Sydney he had his nose smashed in – good practice for his Changi years. But rather than leave the field, he broke a toothbrush, shoved the two bits up his nostrils and led the Wallabies to a rare victory over the All Blacks.

Occasionally referees are forced to invent a law. During the 1960s, in a match involving the Weston-Super-Mare Hornets' Third Fifteen, a Hornets' prop broke wind as a scrum went down. A horrible smell that might have come from a draught-horse after a feed of onions perfumed the surroundings. The prop was warned. But he broke wind again. The referee awarded a penalty against the Hornets, thereby creating a new offence in rugby – the production of foul air.

Gerald Davies argues (correctly, I believe) that the tension between strict liability rugby law and the advantage-oriented spirit of playing the game is one of its attractions: 'One of the perverse charms of rugby football is that the laws are so complicated the game is not clear-cut in any way at all. Why does a scrum collapse? Whose fault is it? Why has a penalty been given? Why was it a free kick and not a penalty? ... Breweries have made their fortunes on after-match post-mortems. The game gorges itself on such talk.'

The website *www.planetrugby.co.uk* devoted three pages of intense discussion to an incident in the 2003 New Zealand–England test at Wellington. The incident lasted probably three seconds, but the post-mortem is endless. England had lost two forwards in the sin bin and faced a scrum on their try line. This sequence of play follows. The six-man England pack is penalised for a prop pushing in at an angle. Rodney So'oialo, the All Black number 8, taps the ball, picks up and drives for the try line. He is stopped at the line by two England defenders. The All Blacks are penalised on the advice of the TMO (television match official) for So'oialo trying to rabbit across the line after being tackled short.

But was this decision correct? Here the complicated laws of rugby come into play.

The website host asks this pertinent question: 'Why weren't the All Blacks awarded a penalty try when So'oialo, after taking a tap penalty, was tackled by players who had not retired to the goal line?'

Law 21.7, What the Opposing Team Must Do at a Penalty Kick, with this section having four parts to it, is then discussed by the website host. The discussion goes into the crucial matter of where the feet of the defenders were. If they were not *behind* the try line before they came forward to make the tackle, the defenders could have committed a 'professional foul', a sin-binning offence. The referee could then have sent both players from the field, leaving England with eleven players. Or he could have given a penalty try. Law 10.2, Unfair Play, covers this option. The key judgements here are whether the defenders 'intentionally' offended and whether a try 'would otherwise have been scored'.

All these considerations had to be weighed up by the referee in seconds – and for hours by the good watchers in the endless post-mortems that follow. No wonder the Welsh have a saying: 'The game starts after the final whistle.'

'Boys from the working-class backgrounds see no point in learning anything when there is a chance that football will toss them 50,000 pounds a week. Rugby, by contrast, is part of an education. The boys that play it are more likely to grow up confident, well-behaved, popular and trusted.'

William Langley, *Sunday Telegraph* **(UK)**

Ultimate team

LIKE THE CATHOLIC concept of the community of saints, there is a community of players and watchers of rugby – the rugby tribe. 'Saint All Black pray for us,' M. K. Joseph wrote in his satirical masterpiece, *A Secular Litany*. All those men and women who played and watched rugby so many years ago, those players and watchers now, and those who will play and watch in the future, are part of the rugby tribe.

Some members include Pope John Paul II, who played rugby in Poland as a young man, and Ernest Rutherford, New Zealand's Nobel Prize winner for splitting the atom, who was an enthusiastic player at Nelson College.

Ernesto 'Che' Guevara, the guerrilla who put chic into terrorism, was a centre who should, perhaps, have played on the extreme left wing. He took up rugby when studying medicine in Buenos Aires in the 1950s and was so infatuated he started his own rugby magazine, *Tackle*. On the other end of the political spectrum, Albert Speer, Hitler's architect, claimed that rugby was his favourite sport. The sport was popular in Germany between the wars, with the national side defeating France occasionally. This success may have inspired Oswald Mosley to call rugby 'a really fascist game'. Perhaps this slur on the rugby ethic is what attracted Romanian dictator Nicolae Ceausescu to play the game. Another well-known despot, Idi Amin, was in the reserves of the East Africa XV which lost 39–12 to the 1955 Lions. Journalist Allan Hogan recalls interviewing Amin when he was dictator of Uganda. Hogan was met at the airport by Amin's adviser Bob Astles, a short, portly Englishman, who was sporting the black tie with silver fern of the New Zealand Rugby Union.

At least three presidents of the United States have had a connection with rugby. Woodrow Wilson, when a college president, tried to turn American colleges to the code, rather than its rival soccer. 'Rugby has a great advantage over the association game,' Wilson orated, 'and all the croakers in our midst must be silenced!'

Current office-holder George W. Bush played fullback at Yale. And, although JFK never took to the field, his brother Teddy played in the centres as a student.

Bill Clinton, a Rhodes Scholar in 1967, the same year as All Black halfback Chris Laidlaw, was an ungainly but enthusiastic second-rower on the playing fields of Oxford. When, as President Clinton, he arrived in New Zealand a quarter of a century later, the first thing he said to Prime Minister Jim Bolger was, 'How's my friend Chris Laidlaw?' Bolger, a former rugby hooker (as was another National Party prime minister, Sir Keith Holyoake), was not amused: Laidlaw was a Labour MP and Bolger was leader of the National Party.

Holyoake and Bolger, with their rugby background, were following the shrewd tradition of Richard Seddon, prime minister of New Zealand when the national side played its first test against Australia in 1903, who rejoiced in the nickname 'The Minister for Rugby'. George Forbes, prime minister of New Zealand in the 1930s, had captained the Canterbury provincial side in 1892. Historian, legislator and diplomat William Pember Reeves, author of the first history of New Zealand and a memorable poem about George Nepia, also played representative rugby for Canterbury as a young man.

Kim Beazley, another Rhodes Scholar and later leader of the Australian Labor Party, was part of a similar tradition of Australian politicians being rugby players. The first prime minister, Edmund Barton, played in the centres. Ben Chifley, famous for his 'light on the hill' vision, was a dashing loose forward. So, too, was the former deputy prime minister, Doug Anthony. Burly Mark Latham, elected Labor leader in 2003, is a coarse rugby fanatic and a dedicated singer of the songs, many of them bawdy.

Literary types, too, have been rugby players. Poet Rupert Brooke was outstanding in the centres at Rugby School. The school magazine described his play: 'Though not brilliant, usually in his place and makes good openings but tackles too high.' Other Rugbeians include Charles Dodson (aka Lewis Carroll) and Salman Rushdie. Another World War I poet, Robert Graves, was a fullback for the First Battalion of the Royal Welsh Fusiliers in a match played in France during the war.

Novelist Bryce Courtenay was a small but lively winger in the then Transvaal, where he played in a curtain-raiser before the South Africa–New Zealand test in 1949. New Zealand playwright Bruce Mason played as a winger in the navy during the Second World War. His brother was an All Black. The 1991 film of Mason's one-man play, *The End of the Golden Weather*, featured Steve McDowell, the mobile All Black prop, running up and down the mythical beach at Te Parenga carrying rocks to build himself up.

Greg McGee, the author of the dramatic rugby play *Foreskin's Lament* and a rangy loose forward, had an All Black trial. Dan Davin, the novelist and famous expatriate New Zealander who developed the Oxford University Press, sported a broken nose – a rugby accident – throughout his life. Dylan Thomas and his wife Caitlin stayed with Dan and Winnie Davin for a week at Oxford and borrowed a couple of rugby jerseys to sleep in, the light blue of Otago University for the poet, and the red and white of Balliol for his wife.

Novelist Maurice Gee played centre and wing as a young man in Auckland. His first novel, *The Big Season* (1962), concerns the repercussions of a murder in a small New Zealand country town, where the residents are more obsessed with the fortunes of its rugby team than the crime that's taken place in their midst. Gee prefers rugby to cricket. 'I like to watch rugby as a spectacle,' he told an interviewer. 'I know this sounds pretentious, but there is something almost beautiful in rugby when it's played properly. You can see the patterns and the movements and you almost appreciate it aesthetically.'

Sir Arthur Conan Doyle gave his famous detective Sherlock Holmes the case of 'the missing three-quarter' to solve. The character of the dashing and missing centre was based on the career of R. W. Poulton-Palmer. Heir to a biscuit-manufacturing empire and arguably England's greatest back, Poulton-Palmer captained England in the 1914 international between England and Scotland, won 16–15 by England. This was the last international played in the northern hemisphere before the outbreak of the First World War, in which Poulton-Palmer, several of the forwards and the majority of the backs in the English team lost their lives.

Rugby has also attracted some notable thespians. Donald McIntyre, the world's first choice for Wagnerian bass-baritone roles, was a tigerish number 8 in the Mount Albert Grammar First XV. Boris Karloff, when not terrifying youngsters in horror movies, was the secretary of the Southern California Rugby Union. Gerard Depardieu, the broken-nosed French film star with the build of a prop forward, is passionate about rugby. In the film *The Closet*, a comedy about a worker who tries to save his job by claiming to be gay, Depardieu plays the part of a rugby coach. As he casts a cynical glance towards his shambling squad of players, Depardieu comments: 'How can we defeat the All Blacks and the Springboks when they have the Super 12?'

Richard Harris cherished the days he played in the Munster Under-20s more than his triumphs on the screen and in the theatre. He was buried in his Munster jersey. Richard Burton had an unrequited ambition to play for Wales as a loose forward. He wrote up his rugby experiences in *A Welcome in the Valleys*. Spike Milligan, a fullback in his army days, had a special admiration for the All Blacks. He desperately wanted to test himself by tackling one of the 'unsmiling giants'. In the Shelbourne Hotel, after the All Blacks had defeated Ireland once again, Milligan saw his chance. Leaning on the bar about 20 metres away, with his back turned to the other drinkers, was the great All Black flanker Ian Kirkpatrick. Milligan gathered himself into a battering-ram position, raced across the room and hurled himself at the unsuspecting Kirkpatrick. His shoulder smashed into Kirkpatrick's back, with great violence. Milligan bounced metres off and tumbled to the carpet. The drink that Kirkpatrick was carrying in one huge fist did not spill a drop. 'Geez,' Milligan wheezed as he pulled himself up from the carpet, 'these All Blacks are men of iron. No wonder we can't beat them.'

Another comedian, John Clarke, creator of the satiric Kiwi character Fred Dagg, wrote a letter as a kid to All Black Terry Lineen. The reply, with a signed autograph sheet of the All Blacks, made Clarke an All Black fan for life.

Stephen Fry, the English actor and director, is a rugby fanatic. Robin Williams is another showbiz personality who loves the All Blacks. Jonah Lomu made a special trip to Los Angeles to present him with an All Black jersey. Williams' riff on the experience was memorable: 'It is so freakin' brutal. I met Jonah Lomu. I never knew how huge he was. I felt like a peasant in a Godzilla movie: "Quickly! Tell the other villagers, we go now!" I realised that I could fall out of Jonah's nose and he wouldn't even know.'

The president of the Victorian Rugby Union, Bill Gillies, has made a hobby of putting together a XV of famous former rugby players. Not unexpectedly, his team has a distinct Australian orientation, although the spread of their chosen professions is impressive. Props: Robbie Coltrane, star of the television series *Cracker*, who played prop for Scotland schoolboys, and Oliver Reed, a stalwart of the London coarse rugby team The Entertainers (especially when propping up the bar after the match). If Reed failed to turn up, Sitiveni Rabuka, kingmaker of Fijian politics, former prime minister, and a prop at Duntroon Military Academy, could be asked to play. Hooker: Bill Hayden, Labor leader and governor-general of Australia, who was hooker for the Ipswich police side. Second row: Cardinal Pell of Sydney, who was a rugby player at Oxford – following in the traditions of Archbishop Redwood of Wellington, the longest-serving bishop of his day, who was a lively halfback at St Patrick's College, Wellington.

Patrick White, Australia's Nobel Prize winner for literature, and a cranky curmudgeon, played in the second row as a student at Cheltenham College. Richard Burton and Che Guevara, the breakaways. Number 8: Sir William Deane, judge of the Australian High Court and later governor-general, a student at the famous Sydney rugby school, St Joseph's Hunter Hill. Deane lost the sight of his right eye playing rugby at Sydney University. Halfback: Rod Laver, a handy halfback – but better tennis player – who gave up rugby when he injured his left hand. Five-eighth: another handy tennis player, John Newcombe, who played for the Shore First XV.

Inside centre: Tony Blair, who was deemed the 'most improved' player at Fettes School, Edinburgh. Outside centre: J. R. R. Tolkien, a keen rugby player at Oxford. Wingers: Jacques Rogge, the president of the International Olympic Committee, who represented Belgium in ten rugby tests, and Jacques Tati, a better comedian than rugby player at the Racing Club of Paris, where he played for the thirds. Fullback: Spike Milligan. Referees: Denis Thatcher, once a touch judge in a test match, and Malachy McCourt, author of *A Monk Swimming*, who has refereed rugby matches in New York.

'If passion is not part of the game then basically they can expect my interest to wane. I don't watch it to appreciate the pure aesthetics or ballet of it all, with sweeping backline moves and raking kicks and clever passing. Sure I appreciate it, and indeed applaud it, but what really makes me to want to stay up until three in the morning with all the other rugby tragics is the suicide run through traffic, the monster hits, the tears during the anthems, the no-regard-for-personal-safety leap to take a garryowen, rucking the shit out of prone players, the "trample the dead and the dying" style of play. I want theatre, passion, I want to feel … that this is the most important thing I need to be watching at this time.'

Andrew H, a *Sydney Morning Herald* reader, in an email to sports writer Peter FitzSimons

Most important thing

R ICHARD BURTON'S perspective on rugby as a concoction of ballet, opera and bloody murder now seems romantic and passé. For modern rugby tragics like Andrew H, rugby is an activity as dangerous and exhilarating as bungy jumping – and as fashionable.

This resurgence of rugby saw a remarkable four million Australians (one out of four of the total population) watching the 2003 World Cup final on television at home. There were probably hundreds of thousands more watching on big screens in pubs. Telstra Stadium, where the final was played, hosted about 30,000 beer-swigging

England supporters in huge tented beerporiums. These supporters did not have tickets for the final, they wanted to enjoy the atmosphere. Altogether the swaying and beer-sodden waiters and standers outside the stadium, with the 80,000 people inside, sent 226,000 text messages and made 202,000 mobile calls. Even the Queen got into the action. 'I've just had a text from my nan,' Prince Harry told the England players celebrating their World Cup triumph in their dressing rooms, 'and she wants to give you a party.'

All those thumbs vigorously tapping out text messages represent a modern way of watching rugby. The new information technology allows people to discuss the game while it is taking place. Post-mortems can be made before the body is dead. I sat beside one journalist who, during a World Cup match, gleefully texted a friend to give him a hard time about the inadequacies of his team.

Instead of having to wait until after the match to discuss it, true believers can now give each other running commentaries as it unravels. The narratives of the people at the match (in the case of the World Cup final, the desire of Australia's supporters to retain the William Webb Ellis trophy and of England's supporters to win it for the first time) are then connected with true believers all over the world to produce support of cosmic proportions.

A new condition, Divided Activities Syndrome, is being created. Adam Liberman, in the *Sydney Morning Herald*, described a DAS incident that occurred during a World Cup match between Australia and New Zealand.

He was at the Sydney Opera House. 'The orchestra was playing the Peer Gynt suite, and as they were entering The Hall of the Mountain King with gusto, I heard someone whisper "What's the score?" Some minutes later I heard a stifled "We've scored!" I looked around frantically, without thinking. I thought I could see the edges of a yellow scarf … or was I becoming delusional?'

You can, in other words, watch a rugby match while at the orchestra.

It can't be long before supporters will use their mobile phones and text messages to synchronise their barracking. When an opposing side has an important line-out on defence, a synchronised roar might be enough to drown out the line-out calls, creating confusion and forcing a referee to penalise the thrower for time-wasting. And think of the possibilities for mobilising the home crowd to help their side with 'flash mobbing' − until now only used to organise crowds through mobile phone calls to participate in bizarre street scenes. A logical extension of this would be to organise stunts in the rugby crowd to disrupt the opposition or their coaches.

Already, the new technology has delivered some unexpected pains. As New Zealand supporters at the 2000 Bledisloe Cup final left the Wellington stadium, after Wallaby John Eales had kicked a match-winning penalty nearly five minutes into extra time allowed by the South African referee, Jonathan Kaplan, they found this blunt message on their cellphones: BUGGER!

'The Rules may be modified, and, alas, evaded, but the game in general will never alter.'

A.C. Swan's assertion in his monumental *History of New Zealand Rugby*

Rugby and eternity

ON THE MORNING of the 2003 centenary New Zealand–Australia test at Auckland, I was on a radio panel with Ron Palenski, rugby journalist, historian and administrator. We were being interviewed on the significance of the coming test by Kim Hill. She asked us a fascinating question: 'Would the players of 1903 recognise the modern game?'

Without hesitation we both agreed that they would. The differences were superficial. Players in 1903, for instance, wore their shin pads outside their socks. But the essential elements of the game — scoring tries, converting them, the line-outs, scrums (eight-man at Eden Park, rather than the seven-man pack played by the New Zealanders in 1903), the rucking, the running and the passing, and even many of the tactics like the cut-out pass and the double-around run – were there in 1903 as they were in 2003.

The major differences the players of 1903 would notice would be how much bigger the players were, with modern backs being much taller and heavier than most of the 1903 forwards, and how fast and clever all the players were, forwards as well as backs. The development of bigger and faster players means that the contact element of rugby has become more intense and ferocious than in the past. As Tana Umaga told the Australian referee Peter Marshall after he had punished the Wellington Hurricanes for supposed over-rough play, 'We're not playing tiddlywinks out here.'

And rugby is being played at a faster pace than ever before. Eddie Jones, the Wallaby coach, expects there will be more passing in the 2007 Rugby World Cup (up from 1.6 passes per possession in 2003 to 1.8 in 2007), fewer line-outs and more fun for the spectators. Jones has predicted that players will run about ten kilometres a match, compared with the eight kilometres they put in now. There will be more lateral movement and more tactical kicking. And the ball will remain in play for 35 minutes – five minutes more than the 2003 test average.

More than a decade ago, in 1991, Godfrey Smith

came to the same conclusion. In his introduction to *Take the Ball and Run*, far and away the best anthology of rugby writing, Smith gave this splendid rationalisation of why the game in general never really alters, but improves like a fine wine: 'The game itself mirrors the snazzier image of its gear. It has demonstrably grown faster ... The players have got bigger ... What is more, they play what must be recognised as a much more exciting game. Unlike association football, which changes its rules seldom, rugby football is continually evolving ... The accident of the pig's bladder lends the game its innate unpredictability.'

The game will not only evolve but continue to give life to other variations and deviations. Gridiron, American football, grew out of rugby, as did rugby league, Sevens rugby, women's rugby and touch rugby. Gridiron's evolution took place in the 1890s, when college administrators in the United States became worried about the excessive violence of rugby, which had come to be called 'the undertaker's friend'. The pile-up scrummage was replaced with a line (in fact a line-out) of scrimmage in which the centre passed the ball between his legs to a quarterback. The forward pass was then introduced, to remove the gridiron game even further from the pile-up, ruck and maul of rugby. However the gridiron authorities then made the mistake of trying to protect players from injuries by allowing them to wear 'protective' clothing. The effect of this has been to make the game far more violent and dangerous than rugby: the fact the tackler's body is protected somewhat by padding has led to harder tackling.

There is no doubt, meanwhile, that 'real' American rugby is a sleeping giant in the world game. At the 2003 Rugby World Cup, the Americans fielded the heaviest pack, over 900 kilograms of prime male. When the authorities there get around to introducing gridiron college stars into their national rugby squad, the major rugby nations will be given a fright. The gladiatorial qualities developed by gridiron fit perfectly into the modern game of rugby, which is increasingly becoming more a running and tackling game than the old kicking, running and tackling game.

Women's rugby now has its own World Cup. This is currently held by New Zealand. The greatest threats to the New Zealand hegemony come from England and the United States. There are now more female rugby players in the United States than male players. The physicality of the game appeals to young women brought up with the credo that 'women can do anything'.

There is a beauty in the way women play. In men's rugby, the skill aspects have been overshadowed by raw and sometimes unskilled power. When the power is taken out of rugby, as it is when women play it, the game is revealed as clever, quick-witted and skilful. However, as in most aspects of modern life, the women are drawn to emulate what the men do. Hence power is entering women's rugby. It will be only a matter of time before a female rugby player emerges who has the strength, power and pace of a modern male player. Such a woman might then claim a place in the All Blacks, or the Wallabies, or in the England or American teams. There does not seem to be anything in the laws of rugby that insists, for instance, that Bledisloe Cup matches have to be contested by all-male sides.

The Sevens — rugby played with the usual laws but seven players a side and seven-minute halves — is becoming the equivalent of one-day cricket. Invented by a Scottish butcher in 1883 to raise money for his club, the game embodies the Scots' flair for economy and practicality. It is festival rather than confrontation, circuses rather than bread. A topless woman at the 2004 IRB Wellington Sevens tournament was protected by the crowd, who, when the police came to arrest her, directed them to another section of the ground. This is the spirit of Sevens rugby.

The stars of the Wellington tournament were the Kenyans. My wife Judy saw them warming up before their match against Korea. The Kenyans would win easily, she told me. I replied that the Kenyans had no form whereas the Koreans had played competently at a number of Sevens rugby tournaments. 'The Kenyans,' the indomitable Judy reasoned, 'have much nicer legs than the Koreans and much tighter and more attractive butts. They are bound to win.' And win they did. They then went on to defeat the Australians. The crowd was ecstatic, not only because of the victory over the hapless Australians but because the way the Kenyans played – their free-spirited running, their manly tackling and the white-teeth-grinning pleasure they took from the game – was infectious.

Writers have to be careful not to fall into the 'white men can't jump' syndrome, but the fact is there is something wonderful about the way Africans and Pacific Islanders play rugby. For them it is still a sport, not 'another day at the office' as it is for some professional players. This is why it is important for world rugby to maintain the interest of African nations such as Kenya (Morocco, too, has a splendid Sevens rugby tradition) and of Pacific nations such as Samoa, Tonga and Fiji.

More outstanding rugby players have been developed on these small territories than anywhere on the globe. The elemental nature of rugby, the exhilaration of running with the ball and daring the smashing tackle, appeals to the Pacific Islanders. If their interests are looked after by the International Rugby Board, and if a Pacific Island side can be developed, I predict that one of these countries, most likely Fiji or Samoa, will play in a World Cup final before, say, Ireland, Scotland or Wales.

Samoans believe that their country is the centre of the universe. One day it could become the centre of the rugby galaxy. Certainly, if Eddie Jones is right and rugby will be played at a faster rate than ever before, the future will belong to the rugby nations that can produce athletes who jump, run fast and tackle hard, and who love the contest, and the bruises and bumps that come with the clash of bodies. Pacific Island genes have already produced arguably the greatest of all the rugby players of the modern era in Michael Jones. And no one has ever run with such power and effect as his fellow All Black Jonah Lomu; Lomu's performance in the 1995 Rugby World Cup semi-final against England was possibly the finest single match ever played by an individual in the history of rugby. These men are not alone.

'Sport has an extraordinary effect on otherwise sane people. Critical faculties are brushed aside for the glory of the moment and the winning of the contest. Partly it is nationalistic fervour, partly glimpses of beauty offered upon a field. Partly it is the recollection of lost youth, partly the primeval urge of man against man.'

Peter Roebuck, Australian cricket writer

Otherwise sane people

THE ART OF watching rugby, as with most activities in the twenty-first century, is becoming more complex. There has, for one thing, been an intensification of nationalistic fervour. Just look at the way the usually inhibited English supporters went crazy over England winning the 2003 Rugby World Cup. And look, too, at the graceless, sullen way New Zealanders took the defeat of the All Blacks by France in the semi-final of the 1999 World Cup. The hapless New Zealand coach, John Hart, was portrayed on the cover of a leading rugby magazine in a mug shot that made him look like a criminal, and the headline that ran across the top of the cover said simply: GUILTY!

The good watcher needs to keep his or her sanity and good humour amid the ballyhoo and the hype. The game and its beauty must be appreciated, as well as the tribal contest that is at its heart. I approached three fellow rugby tragics – Hugh Dillon, a Sydney magistrate; Inky, a colourful columnist for the New Zealand Rugby Union website; and Kevin Roberts, Worldwide CEO of the advertising company Saatchi & Saatchi and former member of the New Zealand Rugby Union board – for their thoughts on how to watch a game of rugby.

In keeping with the imperatives of the new technology, the discussion was carried out by email.

Spiro Zavos to Hugh Dillon and Inky: 'I'd like you to comment on what you think are the basics of the art of watching rugby. One thought I have is that you need to have passion, knowledge and a devotion to your cause and team so that you bring your own intense personal stories to the match … I would argue that the more complexity and stories a supporter brings to a match, either at the game or watching on television, the greater will be her or his enjoyment.

'I also think that when a vast crowd follows the same story-line – the support for the Wallabies in the World Cup semi-final against the All Blacks, for instance, or support for the All Blacks in New Zealand for a crucial Bledisloe Cup test against the Wallabies – that support can power the home side to victory, in the way huge flows of water crashing over a dam turn the turbines to produce electricity.

'I do not think it is a random development that the tribal commitment of spectators to their teams has intensified recently. Whether it be New Zealand, Australia, South Africa, England or whoever, there has been an increase in the painting of the colours on the faces of supporters. Face paint – what can be more tribal than that?'

HD to SZ: 'We watch rugby tribally, aesthetically, intellectually and fantastically. I think some people also watch it nostalgically. I bet that whenever you wait to watch the All Blacks run out, you remember, if only momentarily, the day you watched your first test. We are all mentally singing the rugby equivalent of "Take Me Down to the Ball Game".

'I agree that each person generally takes a story with them into a particular game. It works in a number of ways. I will watch virtually any team sport and have to choose a side before I take much interest. We are tribal and partisan in our bones.

'My coach in the Under-13As gave us a copy of Charlie Saxton's *The ABC of Rugby*, which I still have. He always sat behind the goalposts (which I note Earle Kirton did when he was a selector for the All Blacks) and still prefers to do so. You can see more of what the forwards are doing from the side, but much more of what the backs are up to from end on.'

SZ to HD: 'Let me stop you there, for you have raised an important technical point – the matter of the best position to sit at the ground. Earle Kirton, with his scarf draped casually around his neck, liked to watch from behind, as you have pointed out. Earle did this to see whether the backs were running in straight lines, or whether they were crabbing across the field and easy targets for defenders to knock over. This is much easier seen from behind than from the side. The French, though, the true rugby purists, will not watch rugby from behind the posts. When the play is away from where you are sitting it is virtually impossible to see what is happening in the torrid forward exchanges. The irony in this approach is that, in terms of strategy, the French divide the rugby field longitudinally. The outside zones are called the zones of penetration. The object of the French style is to move the ball as quickly and neatly as possible to these zones.

'The New Zealand/South African/Australian system places great weight on control of the advantage line. The team that moves the ball forward most effectively, rather than sideways in the French manner, is the team that usually wins rugby matches. The best way to appreciate this advantage-line struggle is by watching from the sidelines.

'About the top of the first stand around the halfway mark is regarded as the best watching position. This is the position generally offered to the journalists. But personally I like to be about the ten-metre line to give a slight angle to the viewing. From this position you can see the advantage-line struggle (and hear the smack of the ferocious tackles), and also get a view of the angles the backs are running.'

HD to SZ: 'The second way of watching rugby (or any sport) is for the sheer aesthetic pleasure. Watching David Campese play, for instance, was always pure pleasure.

'A third way is to learn something I don't know. It is an intellectual pleasure. Watching the Lions play in 1971 was one such experience for me. I then went to a coaching talk Ray Williams gave in 1973, when Australia decided that it needed to do something to get off the mat. He explained British techniques of scrumming and hookers. Things which are commonplace now, such as second-rowers binding between the legs of props, and hookers throwing the ball to make use of the winger, and rolling mauls, were innovations that brilliant people like Carwyn James introduced. That is why people like you and Evan Whitton are really important to rugby watchers like me: you help us to see what is actually happening, to read the Rosetta Stone if you like.

'The final way I watch rugby is in a kind of Walter Mittyish way. When I was a kid of about 15, I remember drawing on the back of one of my exercise books the jerseys I planned to win: First XV, Northern Suburbs, Sydney, NSW, Australia. As it happened I got the First

XV one and one from Melbourne University and that was it. But I am still out there with the Wallabies every time they run out.'

Inky to SZ: 'Spiro, a very good question, to which there is no short answer other than to watch the team rather the individuals.'

SZ to Inky: 'If you identify more with a team than with an individual, the hurt when that team loses must be intense?'

Inky to SZ: 'When the All Blacks lose, it assists perspective. Hell, all those young men have ever done is pull on the jersey and done their best, trying to win games on our behalf. And yet the majority will bag them ruthlessly for their mistakes. The All Blacks' standards are higher than anyone else's, and they expect to be judged harshly by their fans. But their true fans have the capacity for humility, and, like their heroes, give the opposition the respect it deserves. That is the essence of test match rugby. If you start believing for a single instant that the job is done before you take to the park, you are in mortal danger.'

SZ to Inky: 'Is there a difference in watching a team, rather than particular individuals in the team?'

Inky to SZ: 'I watch for how well they understand each other as part of a team: who knows where everyone else is at certain times, who leaves which tasks for others, and who steps up to make the play that counts. When they support each other and understand each other, their lines becomes clearer and more beautiful and more compelling as a spectacle. The All Blacks play as a team, and there is a magic in that which carries on outwards to include their fans.'

SZ to Inky: 'I think what you are touching on here is the tribal aspect of watching rugby. When, for instance, the All Blacks and the Wallabies play each other in the Bledisloe Cup tests, they represent two tribes of people, like champions in a medieval jousting contest. Would you agree that, when their champion team wins, there is a psychic lift for the tribes that transmutes into other activities in their personal and national lives?'

Inky to SZ: 'When the All Blacks win, you feel as if they have done it for you personally. Your eyes mist up and you can't even make out the individual numbers on jerseys but you see, through the blur, a black wave pounding against the opposition goal line … I have had that moment several times in a game.'

SZ to HD: 'It seems to me we have missed the epiphany element for the good rugby watcher. Inky touches on this with his recreation of the "blind faith" moment. England supporters, for instance, will never forget the moment when Jonny Wilkinson kicked that damned field goal and won the 2003 World Cup for England. I got the same feeling of exhilaration – what John Updike has called (in a short story on golf) a sporting moment as dense as gold – whenever David Campese or Jonah Lomu, or (remember I am an ancient gentleman now) Ron Jarden got the ball and raced at, around and (in Jonah's case) through their opponents.

'This "Wow!" moment happens frequently in rugby and is one of the great joys of watching games at any level and under any circumstances, anywhere.'

HD to SZ: 'I agree with your epiphany moment idea. I am one who can truly claim to have been present to see David Campese play for Australia Under-21s vs. the Junior All Blacks in 1981, when he made everyone say, "Who is that?" and scour our programmes. Or to see NSW Country beat Sydney with the last play of the game: the up-the-jumper play.

'For me, one of the truly epiphanic moments was seeing Gerald Davies in 1969 score the winning try for Wales against the Wallabies, who had looked for most of the match like beating them. Davis was like a wisp of smoke and Arthur McGill, no mean tackler, was left clutching air as Davies went around him like an antelope fleeing a lion. These were glorious moments. Carlos Spencer's flick between his legs to Joe Rokococo was one such magical moment in the 2003 World Cup.'

SZ to Kevin Roberts: 'Kevin, you have a singular perspective on how to watch rugby. You've marketed the game for Steinlager. You've been a board member of the NZRU. Your company, Saatchi & Saatchi, does its advertising. You live in New York and come back to New Zealand once a month. How do you get to watch any rugby with this hectic business life?'

KR to SZ: 'Living in New Zealand, New York and St Tropez and on the world's finest airlines means having to put in place top-class preparation and scheduling for Big Rugby. [British television sports channel] Setanta delivers live Tri-Nations in the noisy, Pommy/Irish New York pubs on Second Avenue, populated for these games exclusively by Steinlager-drinking Kiwis, Fosters-swigging Aussies and Castle lager louts, all at 10.00 a.m. on a New York Saturday, accompanied by a big fry-up of black pudding, bacon, Irish sausage and fried egg. With three Kiwi mates our pre-match prep is complete. We're ready for the first big challenge. Will the commentary be the knowledgeable experts, or the one-eyed, over-exuberant Aussies or, worse still, the impenetrable Africans?

And then we will the game to unfold in line with our passionate (and very well-informed) hopes. Mobiles are used at half-time to communicate with mates actually at the match, all of us willing the ref, the players (and the wobbly opposition) to get on board with our predetermined plot, a 35–17 All Black victory. Then Saturday afternoon unfolds into a deluge of poor expat Poms flooding into the Premier League soccer. We head back downtown, pleased with our great backs and our win. Or retreat into gloomy despair and a lost weekend if Eales is playing!!!'

SZ to KR: 'We tend to forget that it has only been in the last decade or so, especially with the spread of satellite television, that rugby matches can be watched anywhere in the world while being played. This is a tremendous change. Even in my lifetime, before television, you had to be at a match if you wanted to watch it. In 1956, for instance, the local movie houses used to play 20-minute highlights of the tests of the Springboks' tour. Because the person filming the match − there was generally only one camera − had only a certain amount of film, which had to be conserved, unexpected tries were often missed. Or we "watched" the tests through the radio broadcasts. We had to rely on the rugby writers to tell us how good Ron Jarden or Bob Scott or, going back into the early days of international rugby, Dally Messenger and Billy Wallace were. Your account reminds me that the eras of the rugby writer and the television commentator are over. We now have the era of the universal rugby watcher.

'Your comment about using your mobile to gee up friends at the match is interesting too, because I have a feeling that something to do with text-messaging will be the next advance in watching rugby.

'I have friends who tell me that they have to watch a game live on television, even if it is in the middle of the night, because they feel that they can exercise some power over the outcome with their concentrated will. Do you have other rituals to influence the outcome of a match?'

KR to SZ: 'I feel I have to play my part for the team when I watch rugby matches in New Zealand. This means being there. Regardless of the weather, I wear a long, woollen, 1938 All Blacks' scarf T. P. McLean gave me. His brother was awarded it on his All Black tour. Then it's the Adidas black stadium jacket and off to the traditional pre-match gathering spots to meet up with friends, old players, coaches, and again will the game plan. (Same one as always, dominate up front, magic from Carlos and gas out wide.) Easy. Then the celebrations with 40,000 best friends and a weekend where all is right with the world !!!!'

'You can never understand rugby unless you've watched it played by six-year-olds on cold winter mornings on hard suburban football grounds. You can never comprehend the absurd spectacle of grown men running to and fro for 80 minutes hurting each other and getting dirty in pursuit of a little oval ball unless you have watched little boys in junior teams play the game. It is how they learn to overcome fear and pain. It is how they learn to be noble, for the good of the team, to voluntarily subsume raw individual ambition and submit to the rules of the game. It is how they learn to be men.'

Columnist Miranda Devine in the *Sydney Morning Herald*

True believers

THE OPENING WORDS of the All Blacks' haka, 'Ka mate! Ka mate!' ('It is life! It is life!') encapsulate Miranda Devine's point. Rugby, like other grand theatrical adventures, gives the illusion to players and watchers of living another life. It transcends the real world by creating a new, more emotionally-charged virtual reality.

Bob Stewart, associate professor at Victoria University of Wellington's Department of Human Movement, Recreation and Performance, divides the devotees into four main groups:

Aficionados: Loyal to the game rather than to any team, and enjoy highly skilful matches.

Partisans: Loyal to one team and won't mind if the full-time whistle sounds early if their team is leading. They attend matches as part of an urban crowd, with a commitment akin to religious faith.

Theatregoers: Consider rugby a source of entertainment, like the cinema or the zoo.

Champ Followers: Support a fashionable or champion team or individual from season to season.

In my view, the good watcher should be a combination of the aficionado, the partisan and the theatregoer, but never a champ follower. The basic instinct of the good rugby watcher is tribal, and the basic virtue of the tribe is loyalty.

The reader might like to place these rugby fanatics into the groups identified by Professor Stewart:

Item 1: A journalist sat beside a young boy during the 2003 World Cup semi-final between New Zealand and Australia. Early on, the youngster, who was wearing an All Black jersey, kept shouting out for Joe Rokococo, the sensational try-scoring All Black winger. The youngster left his seat at halftime, when Australia was leading, and returned wearing a Wallaby jersey. For the next 40 minutes he shouted out encouragement to Stirling Mortlock, the hard-running Wallaby centre.

Item 2: A father died after jumping off a pier at Brighton while celebrating England's win in the World Cup final. Anthony Owers, 27, a former lance-sergeant, was dragged under by the current.

Item 3: Jonny Wilkinson may never watch a replay of his match-winning drop goal in the World Cup final. 'It just doesn't appeal,' he told readers in a newspaper column. 'I've got those memories in my mind and they're good enough.'

Item 4: Keith White of Sydney told reporters about a Qantas flight from Hong Kong on the morning after England had defeated Australia in the World Cup final: 'All the cabin crew were hoarse with barracking for Australia the previous night. As we were taxiing out, the captain came over the intercom, graciously congratulating the English team on their victory, then threatening to personally come back and handcuff any English supporters who gloated!'

Item 5: Kerre Woodham, extroverted New Zealand broadcaster, explained how she gave up heavy drinking: 'It was the day the All Blacks lost to South Africa. My partner and I had been out the night before and were too hung-over to drive to Hamilton to see my recently widowed mum. I felt a deep loathing for myself. We chartered a limo with a TV so we could watch the footy, and when we got there my brother offered me a drink. Because I thought the All Blacks had played as embarrassingly badly as I had behaved, I announced, "I'm not going to have another drink till they win by 20." And bugger me, they lost five games in a row.'

Item 6: The Australian eBay auction site before the World Cup Australia–England final had three pages of listings for final tickets. The New Zealand eBay auction site had only two listings. One read: 'Two tickets seated together to the rugby world cup final, Saturday 22nd Nov 2003, 8pm. This event is completely sold out. Don't miss the opportunity … F*%@ing All Blacks.'

So, yes, uninhibited tribalism is at the heart of rugby-watching. Character is required, and displayed, by players and watchers. The tribe hangs together tightly when things go wrong, and when things go well it celebrates together. A victory is a victory for the tribe, not the individual, even though individual brilliance may be its cause.

The good watcher must bring a competitive attitude to the game but never a destructive one. Through thick and thin, the tribe remains forever loyal. As David Kirk wrote in the *Daily Telegraph* (UK) of the All Blacks' defeat by the Wallabies in the semi-final of the 2003 World Cup: 'Do not, repeat do not, continue reading in the expectation that I will somehow discover humility. I know the All Blacks were well beaten but I cannot bring myself to admit gross misjudgement to anyone, let alone a bunch of unknown readers 10,000 miles away. Write to the editor, call me a bad loser, whatever. Do your worst,

I don't care a continental. We lost, we're losers. There, I've said it, that's as good as it gets.'

In 1972 a group of us who played social rugby at the Osterley club in London went up to Cardiff by train to watch Wales play the All Blacks at the famous Arms Park. The Welsh members of our group sang their hearts out as the train raced towards Cardiff. The most enthusiastic singer was Roy Evans, a sausage-maker by trade, a lovely man and a fanatical rugby supporter. Roy had named his house Whineray after the famous All Black captain, whom he admired greatly. After the match, won against the predictions and the run of play by the All Blacks, we went to the Angel Hotel, a pub opposite the ground, where a large crowd had gathered to discuss the test. About an hour or so into the drinking and the discussion I noticed Roy grab my wife, Judy, by the lapels of her coat and then, ashen-faced, stagger away into the men's toilet. I raced in after him.

'Roy, Roy,' I asked him, 'what did Judy say to upset you?'

Roy, still ashen-faced, gave me a frantic look. 'Judy is a lovely girl,' he replied, 'but I almost hit her out there. Do you know what she said? Have you any understanding of what she said?'

'Roy, what could she have possibly said to have provoked you this strongly?'

'She's lovely girl but she said to me, "Roy don't worry about Wales losing, it's only a game."' He shuddered at the enormity of the remark. He gave me a look of great passion and sadness. 'It isn't just a game, you know.'

'The ball comes back, Matt Dawson lets a few seconds tick away and the ball is hoofed into touch and it's all over. Unbelievable. One minute you're thinking about winning the kick-off, keeping the ball, not making a mistake, what to do next. The next, the World Cup is over. One second it couldn't be any more exciting, the next ... all gone.'

Martin Johnson, England's inspirational captain, on the elusiveness of happiness after his team's victory in the 2003 Rugby World Cup final

Heavenly game

THAT EXQUISITELY SWEET moment of triumph may, as Martin Johnson says, disappear almost as soon as it is experienced, but there is a lasting after-glow to famous victories. A play has even been written about Munster's defeat of the All Blacks in 1978. When the All Blacks toured the British Isles that year, they had already demolished a number of national and regional sides and seemed to be unbeatable. On 31 October they met Munster, a provincial side made up of players from clubs in the western and southern regions of Northern Ireland. The All Blacks looked set to add another annihilation to their record of success. After all, from the time of the first national tour to the British Isles in 1905, no New Zealand side had lost a match in Ireland. Or, to put the matter into the local perspective, no Irish side, regional or national, had defeated the All Blacks in 73 years.

But on a misty, cold afternoon, when the breath of the crowd poured from their mouths like smoke from a thousand chimneys, the unhappenable happened. Not only did Munster defeat the All Blacks, they kept the New Zealanders scoreless.

John Breen, a local actor and playwright, was so taken with the mythology and stories that erupted from this match that he interviewed many of the players (including a good-humoured Stu Wilson, one of the play's leading characters) and locals. Their memories of what has become a famous rugby day have been forged into a tremendously funny and energetically-mounted homage to a burning moment in Munster folk history. A cast of six actors play 60 characters (such is the range of the play) in order to tell the story of Munster's historic victory.

The Irish joke is made funnier — for the Irish — because, every time the play is put on, an Irish team gets to defeat the All Blacks. The thrill of winning a World Cup might be already 'all gone' for Martin Johnson but, for the Irish, Munster's famous win is now part of their literature of memory.

Such immortality is fitting: rugby prides itself on being the eternal game. This is celebrated in a particularly effective way in the village of Larriviere, deep in the lush southwest of France, where there is a small chapel called Notre Dame du Rugby, Our Lady of Rugby. In one of the stained-glass windows, below the central figure of the Virgin Mary, a rugby scrum is depicted. In another window Mary cradles an injured player, Pieta-style. And in another she has the infant Jesus in her arms, holding a rugby ball. At the feet of the Virgin and Child, players are jumping in a line-out and Jesus, in the figure of a man, is throwing in the ball.

Jesus is a rugby player!

ACKNOWLEDGEMENTS

Quotations and information have been taken from the following books and newspapers: *Muddied Oafs: The Last Days of Rugger* by Richard Beard (Yellow Jersey Press, 2003); *Take the Ball and Run: A Rugby Anthology* selected by Godfrey Smith (Pavilion Books, 1996); *Art and Its Objects* by Richard Wollheim (Cambridge University Press, 1992); *A Man's Country?* by Jock Phillips (Penguin New Zealand, 1987); *History of New Zealand Rugby* by A. C. Swan (Moa Publications, 1992); *Pick Me Up and Run* by David O'Neil (1995); *The World of Rugby: A History of Rugby Union Football* by John Reason and Carwyn James (BBC, 1979); *The Sydney Morning Herald*; *The Australian*; *The Dominion Post*; *The Sunday Telegraph* (UK) and *The Daily Telegraph* (UK).